The Life of St Brendan and His Prayer

Founder of monasteries, navigator of fantastic voyages, wonder-working inter-cessor and confessor, Saint Brendan of Clonfert and Ardfert (c 486–578) was among the most colourful and celebrated figures of medieval Ireland.

Brendan's renown, nurtured by his monastic community and their princely patrons, approached that of Patrick, Brigit, and Columba, Ireland's national saints. His fame was such that stories about him were told with those of King Arthur and other worthies.

The chief surviving memorials in Latin to Brendan's life, legend and histor-ical influence are three: the *Vita Sancti Brendani* recounting his clerical activities in Ireland and abroad, the *Navigatio Sancti Brendani* relating his fabulous seven-year voyage seeking a terrestrial paradise on the great ocean, and the *Oratio Sancti Brendani*, a lengthy prayer for protection and deliverance that is attributed to him. Definitive versions of these three works have been preserved in two manu-scripts dating from the fourteenth and the eleventh centuries respectively.

This complete translation of the *Vita Sancti Brendani* (from Oxford, Bodleian Library, MS Rawlinson B 485, a version which incorporates the *Navigatio*), and of the *Oratio* attributed to him (from Munich, Bayerische Staatsbibliothek, Clm 13067), offers the first full portrait in English of Brendan not only as the saintly hero of the popular *Navigatio* but also as an emblem of the Gaelic people, their struggles and their aspirations over the long arc of Irish history.

Mediaeval Sources in Translation 62

The Life of St Brendan and His Prayer

Translated with an Introduction and Notes by
GORDON BARTHOS

Toronto

PIMS

PONTIFICAL INSTITUTE OF MEDIAEVAL STUDIES

Acknowledgments

The publication of this volume was made possible by funds generously provided by the Basilian Fathers of the University of St Michael's College.

Library and Archives Canada Cataloguing in Publication

Title: The life of St Brendan and his prayer / translated with an introduction and notes by Gordon Barthos.
Other titles: Container of (expression): Vita sancti Brendani. English
Names: Barthos, Gordon, editor, translator. | Container of (expression): Brendan, Saint, the Voyager, approximately 483–577. Oratio sancti Brendani. English. | Pontifical Institute of Mediaeval Studies, publisher. | Bodleian Library. Manuscript. Rawlinson B 485. | Bayerische Staatsbibliothek. Manuscript. Clm 13067.
Series: Mediaeval sources in translation ; 62.
Description: Series statement: Mediaeval sources in translation ; 62 | This volume includes the translation of Vita Sancti Brendani (from Oxford, Bodleian Library, MS Rawlinson B 485, a version which incorporates the Navigatio), and the Oratio, reportedly attributed to Brendan (from Munich, Bayerische Staatsbibliothek, Clm 13067). | Includes bibliographical references and index.
Identifiers: Canadiana (print) 20230558151 | Canadiana (ebook) 20230558194 | ISBN 9780888443120 (softcover) | ISBN 9781771104340 (PDF)
Subjects: LCSH: Brendan, Saint, the Voyager, approximately 483–577. | LCSH: Christian saints – Ireland – Biography. | LCSH: Christian saints, Celtic – Biography. | LCSH: Bodleian Library. Manuscript. Rawlinson B 485. | LCSH: Bayerische Staatsbibliothek. Manuscript. Clm 13067. | LCGFT: Biographies.
Classification: LCC BR1720.B73 L5413 2024 | DDC 270.2092–dc23

Pontifical Institute of Mediaeval Studies
59 Queen's Park Crescent East
Toronto, Ontario M5S 2C4
Canada
pims.ca

PRINTED IN CANADA

Contents

Acknowledgments

I owe a profound debt to Ann Dooley, Professor Emerita of Celtic Studies and Medieval Studies at the University of St. Michael's College in the University of Toronto, whose deep knowledge of Irish history and culture, and warm encouragement, helped bring Brendan's story to a wider audience. Thanks are due as well to the Pontifical Institute of Mediaeval Studies. Fred Unwalla, then Editor in Chief and now Director of Publications, the Institute's longtime Latin editor Jean Hoff, associate editor Megan Jones, and its peer reviewers, collectively helped define the final text, challenged arguments, and offered invaluable advice. James Carley, Distinguished Research Professor Emeritus at York University, Toronto and Fellow of the Institute, and A.V.C. Schmidt, Emeritus Fellow of Balliol College, Oxford University, saw merit in this translation, and encouraged its publication. The Bodleian Library in Oxford supplied a digitized copy of the manuscript, and the Library of the Pontifical Institute sustained much of the research. Finally, special thanks to Linda Cahill, my cherished spouse and first reader, who took an editor and novelist's interest in Brendan's story from the start and helped shape the telling.

Abbreviations

Anglie	"De sancto Brendano abbate [et confessore]" in *Nova Legenda Anglie: As Collected by John of Tynemouth, John Capgrave, and Others, and First Printed, with New Lives, by Wynkyn de Worde a.d. mdxvi*, ed. Carl Horstman, 1: 136–153 (Oxford, 1901).
AC	*Annála Connacht: The Annals of Connacht (A.D. 1224–1544)*, ed. A. Martin Freeman (Dublin, 1944; repr. 1970).
AFM	*Annala rioghachta Eireann: Annals of the Kingdom of Ireland, by the Four Masters, ...*, ed. and trans. John O'Donovan, 7 vols (Dublin, 1851; repr. New York, 1966).
AI	*The Annals of Inisfallen: MS Rawlinson B 503*, ed. and trans. Seán Mac Airt (Dublin, 1951; repr. 1977).
AU	*The Annals of Ulster (to A.D. 1311)*, ed. Seán Mac Airt and Gearóid Mac Niocaill (Dublin, 1983).
Brussels	Second Irish "Life of Brendan of Clonfert," copied by Mícheál Ó Cléirigh, in *Bethada Náem nÉrenn: Lives of Irish Saints*, ed. and trans. Charles Plummer, 1: 44–95 (Irish); 2: 44–92 (English) (Oxford, 1922; repr. 1997).
Lismore	First Irish "Life of Brenainn, son of Finnlug," in *Lives of Saints from the Book of Lismore*, ed. and trans. Whitley Stokes, 99–116 (Irish); 247–261 (English) (Oxford, 1890; repr. Felinfach, 1995).
LIS	*Bethada Náem nÉrenn, Lives of Irish Saints*, ed. and trans. Charles Plummer (Oxford, 1922; repr. 1997).
M	*Vita* from Marsh's Library in Dublin, in "Vita S. Brendani Clonfertensis e codice Dubliniensi," ed. Paul Grosjean, *Analecta Bollandiana* 48 (1930): 99–123.
NHI	*A New History of Ireland*, ed. T.W. Moody, F.X. Martin, F.J. Byrne, W.E. Vaughan, Art Cosgrove, J.R. Hill, and Dáibhí Ó Cróinín, 9 vols (Oxford, 1976–2011).
R	"Vita prima sancti Brendani abbatis de Cluain Ferta" from MS Rawlinson B 485, Bodleian Library, Oxford, in *Vitae Sanctorum Hiber-*

niae: *Partim hactenus ineditae ad fidem codicum manuscriptorum*
recognovit prolegomenis notis indicibus instruxit, ed. Charles Plummer,
1: 98–151 (Oxford, 1910; repr. Dublin, 1997).

S^1 "Vita prior et navigatio S. Brendani abbatis Clonfertensis" from the
Royal Library of Belgium, Brussels, in *Vitae Sanctorum Hiberniae ex*
codice olim Salmanticensi nunc Bruxellensi. ed. W.W. Heist, 56–78
(Brussels, 1965).

S^2 "Vita altera S. Brendani abbatis Clonfertensis" from the Royal
Library of Belgium, Brussels, in *Vitae Sanctorum Hiberniae ex codice*
olim Salmanticensi nunc Bruxellensi. ed. W.W. Heist, 324–331 (Brussels, 1965).

VSH   *Vitae Sanctorum Hiberniae: Partim hactenus ineditae ad fidem codicum*
manuscriptorum recognovit prolegomenis notis indicibus instruxit, ed.
Charles Plummer, 2 vols. (Oxford, 1910; repr. Dublin, 1997).

Sites associated with St Brendan of Clonfert and Ardfert (map: Adrian Doran)

Introduction

Saint Brendan was one of the most celebrated figures of the medieval era. The chief memorials in Latin to his life, legend, and legacy – the *Vita Sancti Brendani*, the *Navigatio Sancti Brendani*, and the *Oratio Sancti Brendani* – portray Brendan as a saintly hero and as an icon of the Gaelic west who was identified with its people, their struggles, and their aspirations over the long arc of Irish history. Beginning with evidence from the Irish annals for Brendan himself, and proceeding to the surviving manuscript sources, the discussion below touches on the contents, structure, themes, and style of the version of the *Vita* chosen for translation in this volume, one which incorporates the *Navigatio*. The discussion moves on to the *Oratio* attributed to Brendan, reportedly composed when he was at sea, and ends with a note on the translation.

The Historical Evidence

Saint Brendan of Clonfert and Ardfert in Ireland was one of the most renowned and colourful Christian figures of the Middle Ages. According to the Irish annals he was born ca. 486; he died in 578 and came to be memorialized as an abbot, evangelizer, and founder of monasteries during the "Age of Saints."[1] Historically, Brendan's signal achievement was the founding of Clonfert Abbey in Galway, a house on the banks of the Shannon that would flourish for a thousand years. Hailed in the medieval era as a Confessor, a figure of sanctity who endured great hardships for the faith, he came to be afforded a celebrity akin to that of Patrick, Brigit, and Columba, Ireland's national saints. Today, he is better known as the Navigator, or Voyager, alluding to the body of legends that celebrated his travels at sea and nurtured his fame.

1. Richard Sharpe, *Medieval Irish Saints' Lives: An Introduction to Vitae Sanctorum Hiberniae* (Oxford, 1991), 10.

While accounts of Brendan's life owe much to the imagination, his historical origins, his associations, and his foundations are attested in the Irish annals, which, together with hagiographical and genealogical traditions, preserve what Kathleen Hughes memorably described as a "roughly reliable" chronicle of events from about 500.[2] The Annals of Inisfallen record his birth in 486 and death in 578,[3] and according to the Annals of Ulster and Inisfallen, he founded Clonfert between 558 and 564.[4] After his death, the annals consistently refer to Clonfert as Brendan's foundation and name his successors.[5] They even credit him with posthumously defending Clonfert's interests.[6] The annals for 578 also mention a Connacht king, Áed mac Echach of the Uí Briúin Aí, who granted him the land for Annaghdown, Brendan's sister Brígh's convent.[7]

The hagiographic dossier, too, provides evidence of Brendan's existence and his posthumous influence. Oral tales of his sanctity and activities likely spread soon after his death. Cummian's letter from 632/633, *De controversia Paschali*, on the controversy over the dating of Easter, lists a *Brendinus* as one of several *patres meos ... maiores meos* (my fathers and predecessors), and one of the fathers of the Irish church after Ailbhe of Emly and Ciarán of Clonmacnoise.[8] While Brendan

2. Kathleen Hughes, "The Church in Irish Society, 400–800," *NHI* 1: 301–330, at 307. See also Dáibhí Ó Cróinín, "Ireland, 400–800," *NHI* 1: 182–234, at 191; and Clare Downham, *Medieval Ireland* (Cambridge, 2018), 115, 160–161. The Irish genealogists created an extensive record for Brendan, although Pádraig Ó Riain cautioned that "very few if any saints' pedigrees can be regarded as authentic." Ó Riain, ed., *Corpus Genealogiarum Sanctorum Hiberniae* (Dublin, 1985), xv.

3. Seán Mac Airt, ed., *The Annals of Inisfallen: MS. Rawlinson B. 503* (Dublin, 1951; repr. 1977), 62–63, 76–77. The Annals of Ulster place Brendan's death at 577 or 583. Seán Mac Airt and Gearóid Mac Niocaill, eds., *The Annals of Ulster (to A.D. 1131): Part I, Text and Translation* (Dublin, 1983), 88–89, 90–91.

4. *AU* 80–81, 82–83. *AI* 72–73.

5. Clonfert became an important centre soon after its foundation. Maoineann, the first bishop, died in 572. From then, the annals consistently record Clonfert's bishops, abbots, and other clergy, naming scores of them, from Fintan Corad in 592 and Cuimín Fada in 661, to Tomás O Cellaig in 1441. *AI* 78–79; *AI* 94–95; *Annála Cònnacht: The Annals of Connacht (A.D. 1224–1544)*, ed. A. Martin Freeman (Dublin, 1944; repr. 1970), 482–483. Moreover, most of Clonfert's bishops and abbots were Irish up to the abbey's dissolution in 1571.

6. When Clonfert was plundered by the jarl Tomrar from Limerick, the annals for 866 report that "Brénainn killed him [Tomrar]" soon after the raid. *AI* 132–133. Another version says Brendan performed a miracle that caused Tomrar to die from madness. Joan Newlon Radner, ed., *Fragmentary Annals of Ireland* (Dublin, 1978), 122–123.

7. *AI* 76–77. Brendan's other foundations were Inishdadroum and Inchiquin; all his houses were west of the Shannon.

8. *Cummian's Letter De controversia Paschali*, ed. Maura Walsh and Dáibhí Ó Cróinín (Toronto, 1988), 90–91, 90 n262. The identity of Cummian is uncertain; it may have been Cuimín Fada or Cuimín Ailbe of Iona, abbot from 657 to 669. *Cummian's Letter*, 14–15.

of Clonfert may be the figure in question, Brendan of Birr is a possibility; a *Catalogus Sanctorum Hiberniae* from about 750 places *duo Brendani* (two Brendans) in the "second order" of Irish saints, ca. 543–599.[9] The *Martyrology of Oengus*, ca. 800, however, refers to Cummian as "comarba Brénainn Chlúana ferta," in notes that specifically say that the Brendan he succeeded was Brendan of Clonfert, not Brendan of Birr.[10]

In his *Life of Columba*, ca. 700, Adomnán, relying on the testimony of informed and trustworthy elderly men, and on credible oral and written tradition held within the Iona community, twice cites Brendan's repute as a founder of monasteries in the previous generation, and associates him with Columba and his *familia*. One incident has *sanctus Brendenus* visiting Columba at Hinba. During Mass, Brendan reports seeing *quendam criniosum igneum globum et valde luminosum*, a fiery ball of light, around Columba's head. The other mention is of a visitor to Iona, *proselytus Aidanus nomine ... qui ut fertur xii. annis Brendeno ministravit*, that is, Aodhán, a cleric, who had attended on Brendan for twelve years.[11] These early references speak to the genuineness of the Brendan tradition and the prominent place he had among saints of the generation prior to Adomnán.

The *Martyrology of Oengus*, ca. 800, gives Brendan's feast day as May 16.[12] And the ninth-century *Martyrology of Tallaght* refers at March 22 to the *Egressio familiae Brendini*, marking Brendan's setting out to sea.[13] The *Litany of Pilgrim*

9. The "first order" of Irish saints, including Patrick, were missionary bishops from abroad, ca. 440–543; the "second order" were largely native priests who succeeded Patrick and the original missionaries. Arthur West Haddan and William Stubbs, ed., *Councils and Ecclesiastical Documents Relating to Great Britain and Ireland* (Oxford, 1869–1878; repr. 1964), 2: 292–293.

10. Brendan of Clonfert is often confused with Brendan of Birr, but little is known of the latter as no *Life* survives for him. Pádraig Ó Riain notes indications that the two "were originally identical." Ó Riain, *A Dictionary of Irish Saints* (Dublin, 2012), 114. However, Adomnán differentiates the two, relating that both saints had visions of Columba surrounded by light. Adomnán, *Life of St Columba*, trans. Richard Sharpe (London, 1995), 207, 219 [III, 3, 17]. They are differentiated as well in *The Martyrology of Oengus*, the *Corpus Genealogiarum*, and the *Twelve Apostles of Ireland*. Whitley Stokes, ed., *Félire Óengusso Céli Dé = The Martyrology of Oengus the Culdee* (London, 1905; repr. Dublin, 1984), 242–243 n12. Ó Riain, *Corpus Genealogiarum*, 22, item 127.1; 136, item 705.3,4; 140, item 707.35,36; 161, item 712.8,9. According to the legend in *Dá apstol décc na hÉrenn* (*The Twelve Apostles of Ireland*), Brendan of Clonfert was assigned to seek out the Land of Promise because he was "the youngest" of the saints of Erin, although the lot to hazard the ocean journey had originally fallen to Brendan of Birr, the eldest. Charles Plummer, *LIS* 1: 96–102 [Irish], *LIS* 2: 93–98 [English].

11. *Adomnán's Life of Columba*, ed. and trans. Alan Orr Anderson and Marjorie Ogilvie Anderson (Oxford, 1991), 206–207, 52–53 [III, 17; I, 26].

12. Stokes, *Martyrology*, 124.

13. Séamus Mac Mathúna, "The Structure and Transmission of Early Irish Voyage Literature," in *Text und Zeittiefe*, ed. Hildegard L.C. Tristram (Tübingen, 1994), 313–357, at

Saints, also ninth century, names Brendan, his fellow voyagers, and those they encounter at sea.[14] Bili, deacon of Aleth in Brittany, writing the *Vita Sancti Machuti* (the *Life of St Malo*) in 866–872, refers to Brendan as *Brendanus confessor Christi abbas*, makes him abbot of Nantcaruan (Llancarfan in Wales), and says he baptized Malo and schooled him in the faith.[15]

Brendan's medieval Irish hagiographers likened him to Christ, a rare elevation even for Irish saints.[16] From start to finish, his life is replete with wonders, however improbable, that embody a richly creative Irish literary tradition, both religious and secular, whose tales of his sanctity, miracles, and travels appealed to the medieval sensibility, and still evoke interest today.[17]

Manuscript Sources for the *Vita*

The chief surviving memorials to Brendan in Latin are three: The *Vita Sancti Brendani*, recounting the story of his life including his fabulous sea voyage; the *Navigatio Sancti Brendani*, relating the voyage itself; and the *Oratio Sancti Brendani*, a lengthy prayer for protection and deliverance that he is credited with having written during his travels. The *Navigatio* is a well-known "tale of wonders" relating his fabled seven-year quest as a *peregrinus pro amore Dei* (a voluntary exile for the love of God) in search of an earthly paradise in the hidden reaches

---

334. Richard Irvine Best and Hugh Jackson Lawlor, eds., *The Martyrology of Tallaght* (London, 1931), 26.

14. Mac Mathúna, "Structure and Transmission," 334.

15. Bili, *The Old English Life of Machutus*, ed. David Yerkes (Toronto, 1984), 2–6, 30. Carl Selmer, ed., *Navigatio Sancti Brendani abbatis: from Early Latin Manuscripts* (Notre Dame, 1959; repr. Dublin, 1989), xvii–xix.

16. The text translated here recounts pre-birth prophesies of Brendan's greatness, a great light and angels flying in the air on the night he was born, and gifts at his birth from a rich man who is likened to a second Simeon. J.S. Mackley cited Irish texts that provide a pedigree for Brendan which echoes Matthew's genealogy of Jesus as well as Bishop Earc's John the Baptist-like declaration that he will be Brendan's servant. Mackley, *The Legend of St Brendan: A Comparative Study of the Latin and Anglo-Norman Versions* (Leiden, Boston, 2008), 46.

17. Despite its popularity, Brendan's legend had its detractors, including one who, in a thirteenth-century manuscript containing the *Navigatio*, famously observed *O quam stultum et vesanum est de sancto credere* (O how dull and foolish it is to believe the saint). Mario Esposito, "An Apocryphal 'Book of Enoch and Elias' as a Possible Source of the *Navigatio Sancti Brendani*," in *The Otherworld Voyage in Early Irish Literature*, ed. Jonathan M. Wooding (Dublin, 2014), 27–41, at 40. For Dáibhí Ó Cróinín, *Early Medieval Ireland, 400–1200* (London, 1995), 211, the saints' lives are with few exceptions "a dismal swamp of superstition and perverted Christianity, dreary litanies of misplaced reverence and devotion."

of the sea.[18] It was "perhaps the most popular Irish work of the entire middle ages."[19] Versions of these three works are preserved in some 300 manuscripts and fragments, in Latin, Irish, and other languages, attesting to his far-reaching fame and influence.

The origin and dating of the primitive *Vita* and the *Navigatio* remain fraught questions. Scholars have long held that a *Vita* of some kind predated the *Navigatio* and provided material for it.[20] More than a century ago Charles Plummer stated, "We must ... place the composition of VB [*Vita Brendani*], i.e. a Latin life of Brendan containing a voyage narrative differing from NB [*Navigatio Brendani*], earlier than the composition of NB."[21] Séamus Mac Mathúna postulated that the *Vita* or *Vita*-type episodic material served as "workshop fragments" on which the *Navigatio* author partly based the narrative.[22] More recently, Glyn S. Burgess and Clara Strijbosch have concluded that the early Brendan tradition is "undoubtedly of Irish origin," and that "a legend concerning the saint was probably already circulating in the seventh century," possibly containing two versions of a voyage.[23]

As for the dating of the *Navigatio* itself, Carl Selmer believed that it was written by an Irish author in Lotharingia in the tenth century.[24] However, James Carney made the case that it was likely "written in Ireland, by an Irishman, about the year AD 800 or, at most, about a half-century later,"[25] a view that found favour

---

18. Jonathan M. Wooding's introduction to John J. O'Meara's translation in "The Latin Version," in *The Voyage of Saint Brendan: Representative Versions of the Legend in English Translation*, ed. W.R.J. Barron and Glyn S. Burgess (Exeter, 2002), 13–25, at 13.

19. Ó Cróinín, *Early Medieval Ireland*, 230. Giovanni Orlandi and Rossana E. Guglielmetti catalogued 142 Latin manuscripts that contain versions of the *Navigatio*, dating from the tenth century to the seventeenth. Orlandi and Guglielmetti, eds., *Navigatio sancti Brendani: Alla scoperta dei segreti meravigliosi del mondo* (Florence, 2014), cxxxii–cxlvii; and their *Navigatio Sancti Brendani, editio maior* (Florence, 2017), 3. Their edition of the *Navigatio* (2014) is subsequently referenced throughout as the "common" version. Burgess and Strijbosch catalogued eighty-seven vernacular versions from the twelfth century in Middle English, Anglo-Norman, French, Dutch, German, Italian, Occitan, Catalan, and Norse. Glyn S. Burgess and Clara Strijbosch, *The Legend of St Brendan: A Critical Bibliography* (Dublin, 2000), 49–78.

20. Jonathan M. Wooding, "The Date of *Nauigatio S. Brendani abbatis*," *Studia Hibernica* 37 (2011): 9–26, at 25–26; and Mackley, *Legend*, 17.

21. Charles Plummer, "Some New Light on the Brendan Legend," in *Otherworld Voyage*, ed. Wooding, 1–14, at 10.

22. Mac Mathúna, "Structure and Transmission," 333.

23. Glyn S. Burgess and Clara Strijbosch, eds., *The Brendan Legend: Texts and Versions* (Leiden, Boston, 2006), 2.

24. Selmer, *Navigatio*, xxviii–xxix.

25. James Carney, "Review of *Navigatio Sancti Brendani Abbatis*, Edited with Introduction and Notes by Carl Selmer," in *Otherworld Voyage*, ed. Wooding, 42–51, at 49.

with *Navigatio* translators J.F. Webb and John J. O'Meara.[26] Although David N. Dumville advanced a somewhat earlier date, contending that the *Navigatio* was composed before 786,[27] the scholarly consensus is that the *Navigatio* like the *Vita* was composed in Ireland and places the work ca. 800.[28]

By the time Brendan's early *Vita* and *Navigatio* were composed, the tradition of hagiography in the British Isles was well established: Cogitosus wrote a Life of Brigit around 650; Muirchú and Tírechán produced early accounts of Patrick's life by ca. 690; Adomnán wrote his *Life of Columba* by 700; *Lives* of Cuthbert, Wilfrid of Ripon, and Ceolfrith followed.[29] In his account, Adomnán presents Brendan and other saints as worthy of veneration and, it might be inferred, of *Lives* of their own. "The Life of a saint was the subject of legend from the start," as Richard Sharpe has noted, emphasizing sanctity through acts of power.[30] The clerical promoters of saints' lives, cults, and relics, Brendan's included, aimed to glorify their subjects, to assert the prestige and privilege of their houses, to please princely patrons, to address the concerns of their day, and to tell a compelling story that would bolster their income by attracting patronage, devotees, and pilgrims.[31] Brendan's community, like those of other saints, would have composed his story "to promote both the fame of their patron and the authority of his monastic rule."[32]

Despite the venerable age of Brendan traditions, the surviving accounts of Brendan's life are relatively late literary artefacts. Most appear to have been compiled after the Anglo-Normans arrived in Ireland in 1169, and after European religious orders had established themselves there during the monastic revival of the twelfth century. They were thus composed largely in an Anglo-Irish monastic con-

---

26. J.F. Webb, "The Voyage of St Brendan," in *Lives of the Saints* (Harmondsworth, 1973), 20. John J. O'Meara, *The Voyage of Saint Brendan: Journey to the Promised Land* (Gerrards Cross, 1991), x.

27. David N. Dumville, "Two Approaches to the Dating of *Nauigatio Sancti Brendani*," in *Otherworld Voyage*, ed. Wooding, 120–132, at 131–132. Orlandi and Guglielmetti, *Navigatio* (2014), cii, cxiv, citing Dumville approvingly, also favoured an early dating for both, by 800, believing that they were inspired by a lost original which may have been much older.

28. For the works' Irish origins, see Sharpe, *Saints*, 28; and Jonathan M. Wooding, "The Medieval and Early Modern Cult of St Brendan," in *Saints' Cults in the Celtic World*, ed. Steve Boardman et al. (Woodbridge, 2009), 180–204, at 182–183.

29. T.M. Charles-Edwards, *Early Christian Ireland* (Cambridge, 2000), 284. There are upwards of 100 surviving Latin lives of about sixty Irish saints, and some fifty Irish lives of about forty saints. Sharpe, *Saints*, 5–6.

30. *Life of St Columba*, trans. Sharpe, 5.

31. Donnchadh Ó Corráin, *The Irish Church, Its Reform and the English Invasion* (Dublin, 2017), 119.

32. James F. Kenney, *The Sources for the Early History of Ireland: Ecclesiastical* (New York, 1929), 411.

text where manuscripts were written in Latin in an English style gothic script with Irish abbreviations and decorative flourishes, and they share common material.[33]

The *Vita Sancti Brendani* survives in five Latin versions in thirteen manuscripts and fragments from the early fourteenth century to the seventeenth.[34] The most extensive Latin versions of the *Vita* are preserved in three collections of Irish saints' lives. Named for the cities, Oxford, Dublin, and Salamanca, where they are now held, or were formerly, they are designated by Sharpe and others as the *Oxoniensis* collection, which includes the Rawlinson B 485 manuscript that contains the extensive *Vita Brendani* translated here; the *Dubliniensis* collection, ca. 1230, whose surviving manuscripts are from the fifteenth century; and the *Salmanticensis* collection, early fourteenth century.[35] Rawlinson B 485 in the Bodleian Library at Oxford, written around 1300, contains the most developed *Vita Brendani*, which incorporates the *Navigatio*. The text recounts his mixed Christian/pagan parentage, his associations with early kings and saints, his role as the founder of Clonfert and other houses, and his travels and miracles. Bayerische Staatsbibliothek *Codex Latinus Monacensis* 13067 in Munich, written around 1075, contains the *Oratio* (discussed further below), a text drawn mainly from church tradition and biblical sources that attests to his repute as a protector and intercessor. These two manuscripts are indispensable witnesses to Brendan's fame in the medieval era.

This translation, *The Life of St Brendan and His Prayer*, makes accessible to English readers the chief surviving memorials to this saint. They present Brendan as an audience would have encountered him in an era when tales about him were told with those of King Arthur and other worthies.[36] They also speak to the interest his story evokes to this day, when he remains a focus of popular devotion, historical speculation, and scholarly study.[37]

33. Brian Ó Cuív, *Catalogue of Irish Language Manuscripts in the Bodleian Library at Oxford and Oxford College Libraries: Part 1, Descriptions* (Dublin, 2001), 117, 208; and Sharpe, *Saints*, 35, 254–255.

34. Burgess and Strijbosch, *Bibliography*, 4–8.

35. Kenney, *Sources*, 304–307. Burgess and Strijbosch, *Bibliography*, 3. Sharpe dated the composition of the Rawlinson *Vita* to around 1300, believing it to be "coeval with the work of the collector" of the *Oxoniensis* collection, embodying "his own expanded text." Sharpe, *Saints*, 370, 24–25 n89. For further information on the *Dubliniensis* and *Salmanticensis* collections, see the discussion in Appendix 2.

36. Louis Gougaud, *Les Saints irlandais hors d'Irlande* (Louvain, Oxford, 1936), 7, cites the *Roman de Renart*, Branche 1, 2389–2392, twelfth/thirteenth century, in which Renart the fox passes for an Anglo-Norman jongleur who can recite *matière celtique*: "Ge fot savoir bon lai breton / Et de Merlin et de Noton, / Del roi Artu et de Tristran, / Del chevrefoil, de saint Brandan." The Annals of Ulster, for 467, testify to an early Irish interest in Arthurian material: "Death of Uter Pendragon, king of England, to whom succeeded his son, King Arthur, who instituted the Round Table." *AU* viii–ix, 48–49.

37. In the modern period, from 1600 to the Great Famine of the 1840s and beyond, Irish emigrants carried their devotion to Brendan to the United Kingdom, the United States,

The *Vita Sancti Brendani* text from the Oxford collection is found in two manuscripts in the Bodleian Library: Rawlinson B 485, and a copy, Rawlinson B 505.[38] Plummer, who edited Rawlinson B 485, regarded it as "a good deal older" than the copy,[39] which he believed belonged to the monastery of Augustinian canons on Saints' Island in Lough Ree, some 80 km from Clonfert, and found it "probable" that the original belonged there as well.[40] Pádraig Ó Riain, too, believed that the *Vita* was influenced by Augustinians connected with priories established in the twelfth century at "the four Irish centres of the saint's life-cycle" at Rattoo in north Kerry, at Canon Island in the Shannon estuary where the river Fergus joined it, at Annaghdown, and at Clonfert.[41] Clonfert had become an Augustinian foundation by 1140.[42]

Sharpe held that the manuscript was made by an Irish scribe "on the borders of Connacht," where Rawlinson B 485 and its copy "belonged from the start somewhere in the district of Longford or Westmeath."[43] While Sharpe and others believed the Rawlinson B 485 manuscript was compiled ca. 1300–1350, there is no firm consensus on a more precise dating.[44] Plummer, citing other experts,

---

Canada, France, Italy, Australia, New Zealand, and elsewhere, where churches and schools dedicated to him still flourish. To this day, "St Brendan remains the archetype of the Irish exile." Wooding, *Otherworld Voyage*, xi. In Montreal, Canada, the translator's home city, St Brendan's Church was built in 1928/1929 for an English-speaking Irish Catholic community. A modest timber and stucco structure in the shape of an inverted beached ship, its rafters evoke a ship's ribs.

Popular culture has always reflected an interest in Brendan. In 1875, John O'Hanlon gave an extensive account of Brendan's legend in his *Lives of the Irish Saints*. So did Denis O'Donoghue in 1893, in *Brendaniana: St Brendan the Voyager in Story and Legend*. Today, scholarly work on Brendan has swelled into "a complex body of material," as Burgess and Strijbosch, *Bibliography*, vii, noted in their compilation of more than 800 items.

38. Oxford, Bodleian Library, Rawlinson B 485 (formerly Clarendon 41), fols. 72v–91r, fourteenth century; and its copy, Oxford, Bodleian Library, Rawlinson B 505 (formerly Clarendon 53), fols. 101v–116v, late fourteenth century. They comprise what is known as the *Codex Insulensis* transmission of the *Vita*. Sharpe, *Saints*, 247–248.

39. Charles Plummer, ed., *Vitae Sanctorum Hiberniae* (Oxford, 1910; repr. Dublin, 1997), 1: xviii n2.

40. *VSH* 1: xx. Sharpe, *Saints*, 249, cautioned that this connection has not been established.

41. The Augustinians appear to have promoted Brendan's cult in Ireland from the twelfth century. Ó Riain, *Dictionary*, 116.

42. Aubrey Gwynn and R. Neville Hadcock, *Medieval Religious Houses, Ireland* (London, 1970), 64, 153.

43. Sharpe, *Saints*, 255, 265.

44. According to Kathleen Hughes, Francis Wormald dated it to ca. 1350. "A Manuscript of Sir James Ware: British Museum Additional 4788," *Proceedings of the Royal Irish Academy* 55 (1952/1953): 111–116, at 116. Francis J. Byrne described it as early fourteenth century. *A Thousand Years of Irish Script: An Exhibition of Irish Manuscripts in Oxford Libraries* (Oxford, 1979), 19–20.

advanced dates ranging from ca. 1200 to 1400.[45] Burgess and Strijbosch, and Brian Ó Cuív, described it as fourteenth century.[46] Ó Riain proposed 1375–1425.[47]

The Rawlinson B 485 manuscript is compact, measuring 230 mm by 165 mm, with leaves that have two columns of text, and about thirty-seven lines to a column. Largely unadorned, it features a title, *Vitae Sanctorum Hiberniae*, at the top of folio i recto. The manuscript now contains the lives of Brendan and thirty-one other saints in whole or in part, but a list of contents from the fifteenth century suggests that the book once had thirty-nine lives, indicating a loss of some twenty-four folios, along with seven lives. The text is in Latin, in a small, bold gothic script on 160 folio sheets of vellum; Irish appears in conjunction with the text in a few places, and in marginal notes and jottings.[48] The script is heavily contracted.[49]

The *Vita* of Patrick that opens the collection in Rawlinson B 485 is differentiated: It is paginated while the other lives are foliated.[50] In Rawlinson B 485, Brendan's story is the eleventh in a series that begins with Patrick and Columba; it follows Brigit and precedes Ciarán of Clonmacnoise. It begins with a large, rubricated capital F halfway down the second column of text on fol. 72v and ends on fol. 91r. Plummer styled the Rawlinson B 485 account the *Vita prima sancti Brendani abbatis de Cluain Ferta*; its copy, Rawlinson B 505, begins with *Incipit vita sanctissimi Brandani abbatis de Cluanferta*.[51]

The *Vita Sancti Brendani*

The Rawlinson B 485 *Vita Sancti Brendani* has been characterized by Strijbosch as the "most detailed" of Brendan's lives, as it "incorporates the largest number

45. *VSH* 1: xxi–xxii.
46. Burgess and Strijbosch, *Bibliography*, 6. Ó Cuív, *Catalogue*, 115.
47. Pádraig Ó Riain, ed., *Beatha Ailbhe: The Life of Saint Ailbhe of Cashel and Emly* (London, 2017), 43 n17. Also, Pádraig Ó Riain, ed., *Beatha Bharra: Saint Finbarr of Cork: The Complete Life* (London, 1994), 104–113. For a full discussion of dates, see Sharpe, *Saints*, 253–255.
48. Ó Cuív, *Catalogue*, 117.
49. At CII, for example, folio 91r, column A, line 23, reads: *H.n.er rr t. sce di*, with superscript marks, which Plummer expanded to *Hic enim erit resurrectio tua, sancte Dei* (For here will your resurrection be, saint of God). *VSH* 1: 150.
50. Sharpe, *Saints*, 253.
51. *VSH* 1: ix, 98.

of biographical *vita* episodes."[52] For Plummer, the author's "great achievement" is in "preserving for us materials which exist nowhere else."[53]

While not the earliest of Brendan's lives, the Rawlinson account can serve as a foundational text against which to assess other, less comprehensive, versions. Certainly, the compiler appears to take a special interest in Brendan's story. Apart from Patrick's *Life*, Brendan's, comprising some 19,000 words with its near-complete version of the *Navigatio*, is the longest in the collection, affording Brendan a status that approaches that of Patrick himself; it is roughly twice the length of the lives of Brigit and Columba.[54] When *Navigatio* elements are discounted from the Brendan *vitae*, the Rawlinson version runs to some 7,700 words; *Dubliniensis* is 5,000 words, and *Salmanticensis* (W.W. Heist's "Vita altera" in S^2) is 2,000 words. A further life, the *Vita Anglie*, is 1,500 words.

In addition to being the amplest Latin version of Brendan's life in the most westerly collection of saints' lives, closest to Clonfert, the Rawlinson account also goes the furthest in elevating his status. Reworking traditional material that long predated the arrival of the Anglo-Normans in Ireland in 1169, it is more politically and culturally nuanced than other versions insofar as it appears to reference, however lightly, unresolved political, social, and religious concerns of the day. Made at a time when Irish princes were contesting the Anglo-Irish settlement and when the Shannon still served as a frontier, it memorializes Brendan as an iconic saint of the Gaelic west whose story was well-known on the Continent and whose chief foundations were insular, located in regions that retained their Gaelic character in the wake of foreign invasion and occupation, and where the English crown and culture never fully penetrated.

The story of Brendan's life, retold at length in dark and uncertain times, was not merely an attempt to reimagine early Christian Ireland for a medieval audience with a taste for the archaic and the arcane, or to indulge fantasies of escape to a better place. It had powerful contemporary resonance, inviting an Irish audience to reflect upon and to celebrate its secular heritage as well. At one level Brendan's life is a paean to Irish Christianity's salvific power and legitimacy; at another, through his colourful dealings with Irish nobles, their seers and officials, paupers, and others, it affirms the dynamism and worth of secular society. Notably, Brendan's devotees cherished him from early days as a figure who shared their identity and heritage, and who protected their dynasties.

---

52. Clara Strijbosch, *The Seafaring Saint: Sources and Analogues of the Twelfth Century Voyage of Saint Brendan* (Dublin, 2000), 281.

53. *VSH* 1: xxiii.

54. Sharpe, *Saints,* 250–251. Charles Plummer, "On Two Collections of Latin Lives of Irish Saints in the Bodleian Library, Rawl. B. 485 and Rawl. B. 505," *Zeitschrift für celtische Philologie* 5, no. 1 (1905): 429–454, at 430–431.

Importantly in this context, Brendan's roots, and his sphere of activity west of the Shannon, differentiated him from other, national, saintly figures. Patrick, while universally celebrated, was a Romanized Briton, not Irish, whose principal church was in present-day Ulster. Columba was a *peregrinus* identified with Iona in what is now Scotland, where his Life was written. Brigit was historically the chief saint of Leinster in the southeast, where Anglo-Irish influence would be pervasive. Brendan, in contrast, was a saint of the Gaelic west, rooted in Munster and Connacht, where his foundations were located, where his cult flourished, and from whence his fame arose.

Scope and Contents

Before discussing the Rawlinson narrative's structure, themes, and style, a summary of its contents may be of use. The *Vita* appears to be conceived and composed as a triptych. It opens with an account of Brendan's birth and youthful activities, then presents the story of his voyage, and closes with accounts of his later missions and death.

Youthful activities. Brendan is born near Tralee in Kerry, of mixed Christian and pagan parentage, after his mother has a prophetic dream that she will bear a child of great holiness and power (Chapter 1).[55] Marvels attend his birth, he is fostered by a nobleman who receives him as "Simeon the just" received the Christ child and offers rich gifts, and Bishop Earc places him in the care of Íde of Killeedy (2–3). Later, under Earc's tutelage, divine providence answers Brendan's prayers, and he is credited with inspired insight (4). He chastises a royal maiden who tries to distract him from his psalms, and although Earc is displeased, angels attend on the boy, and his face shines with glory (5). His blessing saves a man from pursuers by causing them to mistake him for a standing stone, and to attack a stone they take to be him (6). Brendan draws water from the earth during a drought (7). He converts Colmán of Cloyne (8). He directs Iarlaithe to establish a monastery at Tuam (9). He writes a monastic rule at the command of an angel (10). After Brendan raises a dead youth, evangelizes Connacht, and attracts many followers, Earc confers priestly orders on him (11). Finally, rounding out the story of his youth, he yearns to travel "to a far country," and God in a vision promises to conduct him to a delightful island in the sea (12).

Brendan's voyage. The *Navigatio* opens with Brendan recalling how another holy man, Barinthus, once told him and his followers of his visit to a remote island

---

55. All parenthetical references to the *Vita* refer to the chapter divisions in Plummer's edition of the *Vita Sancti Brendani*, but use Arabic numerals. The word "Chapter" has been added where necessary to avoid ambiguity.

where the monk Ternoc lived before the gates of paradise, and to the nearby *terra repromissionis sanctorum,* the Promised Land of the Saints, a land full of rare fruits and precious gems and watched over by angels. It is the land which God "will give to his saints at the end of time." (13). Brendan and his crew set out to seek that land, stopping at Inishmore to visit Éanna (14). They then go to Kerry to build a light oxhide-skin boat. Three monks ask to join them, and Brendan foretells that the first will find an "exalted place" on the voyage, and the second will obtain grace, but the third will be doomed (15).

Setting out and letting God steer the boat (16), they reach the island of the heaven-sent *fidelis procurator,* here translated Faithful Steward (17). There they find a richly equipped palace where Brendan says a brother will be tempted to sin (18). Satan induces one of the late-coming monks to steal a bridle set with silver (19); Brendan confronts the thief and exorcizes the demon that has possessed him; the brother repents, dies, and is carried to heaven (20). They meet the Steward, who provisions them (21). They then make for the Isle of Sheep, where they celebrate Holy Thursday (22). On Good Friday the Steward tells them that God requires them to celebrate Easter on a nearby island, then to proceed to the Paradise of Birds to await Pentecost (23). The first island turns out to be the monster Casconius, the greatest of sea creatures, that terrifies them with its movement (24). The birds of the next island are fallen angels who "consented in part" but not fully to Lucifer's rebellion, and who congregate there on feast days and Sundays to praise the Creator, who showed them mercy by not casting them into hell. One tells Brendan he will celebrate Easter every year on Casconius during their seven-year travels and then will find the *terra repromissionis* (25–26). The birds praise God, day and night, by singing psalms (27). On Pentecost the Steward again provisions them, and the bird tells them they will spend every Holy Thursday of their travels on the Isle of Sheep, every Easter on Casconius, and Christmas with the community founded by Ailbhe of Emly (28).

On reaching Ailbhe's island they find a monastery where the monks live in silent retreat, mysteriously provisioned through "God's abundant goodness," where they need no fire to cook food or to warm themselves, where old age and feebleness do not trouble them, and where their lamps are lit by divine breath. Although Brendan yearns to remain with them, he is instructed to stay only until the octave of the Epiphany, then to resume his voyage (29–35).

At the start of Lent, marking the beginning of their second year at sea, they are imperilled by a stupor-inducing spring (36), and are becalmed on a curdled sea (37). On Holy Thursday they again reach the Isle of Sheep (38), then celebrate Easter on Casconius (39), and spend the Easter octave at the Paradise of Birds (40), where Brendan is reminded once again that God has ordained four moments in time for them: Holy Thursday with the Steward on the Isle of Sheep,

Easter on Casconius, Pentecost at the Paradise of Birds, and Christmas with Ailbhe's community. Brendan is assured that he will find the *terra repromissionis* after seven years, stay there for forty days, then return to Ireland (41). Setting sail once more (42), they are attacked by a sea beast and through Brendan's prayer are defended by another (43–45), then are marooned for three months (46). They next sail to the Isle of Steadfast Men, where three choirs of monastics sing God's praises continuously and welcome the second late-coming monk to their community (47–50). Sailing again, they obtain wondrous provisions of grapes (51–54) and are attacked by a gryphon and defended by a bird. Finally, they reach Ailbhe's community, rounding out their second year at sea.

The story proceeds to recount heavenly and hellish wonders they encounter during the middle years, three through six, of their travels. On St. Peter's Day they reach waters so clear they can see the monsters of the deep (55), who reverence the Mass. They find a vast crystal column and silver-coloured canopy containing a chalice and paten, and Brendan announces that Christ has shown them such marvels to glorify God's power (56). They reach a terrifying island full of the workshops of demonic smiths. They escape attack, then, "close by the mouth of the infernal pit," come to a mountainous, burning island where demons carry off the third late-coming monk (57–59).

In their final year at sea, as Lent draws near, they reach the island of Paul the hermit, who was raised in St Patrick's community, and who cared for the cemetery where Patrick was buried. One hundred ten years old, Paul is clad only in his own hair, and has survived for decades living only on spring water. He tells Brendan he will soon reach the *terra repromissionis* (60–62). They sail through Lent, spend Easter with the Steward and on Casconius, and spend Pentecost with the birds. The Steward then conducts them "ever to the east," to the fog-shrouded *terra repromissionis*, a land undarkened by night, where Christ is the perpetual light. They remain there for forty days before they make for Ireland carrying away rare fruits and precious stones, first reaching Ternoc's nearby island community (63–66).

At this point the common text of the *Navigatio* ends with Brendan returning to Ireland and dying. However, the Rawlinson account from 67 through 76 amplifies the *Navigatio* by telling additional tales from the *Vita* tradition relating to Brendan's years at sea, seemingly in the form of reminiscences on his return home. Unlike the *Navigatio*, these extensions do not emphasize the liturgical year and appear to be less anchored in a monastic setting. They focus chiefly on delivery from danger and death, on providential guidance, and redemption.

Satan shows himself to them, offering a fatal glimpse of hell to one monk, whom Brendan raises from the dead (67). Upon encountering a dead girl of gigantic size, Brendan restores her to life, baptizes her, and buries her when she chooses death and heaven over mortal life (68). They reach an inaccessible island where they hear singers praising God, but are thrown a wooden message board warning them that this is not the promised land and to continue their search (69). Parched with thirst, they escape death when Brendan advises them to sing hymns to bless streams of water from which they are tempted to drink, revealing them to be poisonous (70).

The narrative, still drawing on the *Vita* tradition, at this point recounts Brendan's return to Ireland after five years at sea (71). There, Íde counsels him to relaunch his voyage in a wooden vessel, fitter for travelling to the holy *terra repromissionis* than their original boat. The new ship is built in Connacht, where a herald joins them. They sail to Éanna at Inishmore, then travel to an island where the herald embraces a form of martyrdom by surrendering himself to huge ravenous rats (72). Later, when their smith dies, Brendan buries him in the sea, where his body remains fixed in the waves as if in an earthen grave (73). Brendan blesses a brother's hands so that he is fit to replace the smith and can make an anchor to replace the one that had become wedged in the rocks (74). In another encounter with an Irish hermit, Brendan's prayer delivers them from the clutches of a monstrous cat. The hermit receives communion from Brendan, then dies (75). Finally, in the last encounter at sea that Brendan recalls, they meet a holy man living in a "paradise amid the waves of the sea," who, in an angelic voice, says he has long awaited their arrival. He tells Brendan to return home to save the Irish from their sins, then dies (76).

Brendan's missions. The Rawlinson text goes on to present an extensive account of Brendan's missions in later life, taken from the *Vita* tradition. Returning to Ireland from his second voyage, Brendan reaches Éanna's islands again, then makes his way back to mainland Ireland and the Shannon, landing at Inishdadroum Island near Limerick (77). When Irish fishers deny Brendan provisions, their waters become barren (78). Brendan cures a pestilential plague of fleas (79), causes the royal settlements of residents who have wronged him to be deserted (80), and entrusts his boat to a boy, whose mistrustful brother insists on taking his place and is drowned when the tide comes in (81). Stricken by remorse, Brendan seeks Íde's counsel, and she advises him to go abroad and gain souls for Christ (82).

Brendan proceeds to Britain to see Gildas (83–85). During his visit, acts of power affirm Brendan's sanctity and authority as an Irish cleric when Gildas puts him to the test: Gates burst open at his command; snow doesn't fall on him; he presides over miracles at Mass, where Greek writings are unveiled to him and Gildas is terrified to see a human finger on the paten at the consecration; and he domesticates lions that had tormented the people. Chastened, Gildas invites Brendan to stay and rule the place, but he replies: "What is the present world to me?"

Brendan travels on, founding a church on a British island (86) where he sees marine beasts battling. When one of them invokes St Brigit's aid, Brendan wonders why he was ignored and returns to Ireland seeking her out. Brigit explains that her mind, unlike his, is ever fixed on Christ. Back in Britain, Brendan founds a church on the Isle of Tiree (87) and foresees heresy in Britain.

On his return to Ireland (88), Brendan infuriates the Connacht king Áed mac Echach by requisitioning the king's horses on Inchiquin Island at Lough Corrib, but the Lord appears to Áed in a dream warning him not to harm Brendan, and the king grants him the island and the horses. Brendan is advised that a monk at Inishdadroum has been slain by a hatchet (89). He summons the dead man to Inchiquin, and the monk arrives with the hatchet still fixed in his head; he chooses to die, and is then buried there. Brendan buys a man and his family freedom (90) by uncovering a mass of gold for their ransom. At age seventy-seven, he founds Clonfert (91), where he raises a dead boy. At Christmas, an angel carries Íde from Killeedy all the way to Clonfert in the blink of an eye to receive communion from Brendan (92). At Múscraige Tire, Brendan urges the people to pray to the virgin St Ciar, who quenches an unearthly fire that has long tormented them (93). On a visit to Brendan of Birr (94), the salt pork served to Brendan and his monks on Good Friday, which scripture and the brotherly rule enjoin them to graciously accept, is later found to be pure bread, so that they do not break the fast.

Brendan then meets King Diarmait mac Cerbaill (95), who in a dream sees his golden chain being given to Brendan, signifying that the reign of pagan high kings is at an end. Brendan tells the tale of Earc's cherished bronze cup, abandoned on Casconius' back on their first Easter at sea and miraculously recovered on a subsequent visit (96), and recalls encountering Judas on a rock in the sea (97). He recounts the tale of a man from Corcomroe (98) who fled his quarrelling wives and tells of an island supported by columns tall enough for ships to pass under (99). He redeems the irascible monk Colmán from torment after death (100), demonstrating the efficacy of prayer for the dead.

Brendan subsequently saves Connacht from attack by the kings of Munster (101), and cures a man who was mute. Finally, at his sister Brígh's community at Annaghdown (102), he foresees his death and the circumstances surrounding it. He dies, at ninety-three (103), and is carried to heaven as the angels rejoice. The text asserts, wrongly, that the *Life of Columba the Abbot* relates that Columba foresaw Brendan's death and had solemn Mass said for him (104). Finally, when all Brendan has foretold has come to pass (105), his body is carried to Clonfert and buried.

As this outline indicates, the Rawlinson narrative links Brendan to many of Ireland's early saints, including Patrick, who died 457/461 or 493 (Chapter 62), to Brigit of Kildare in Offaly (452/456–524/526; Chapter 86), and to Columba of Iona (521–597; Chapter 104). Brendan's tutor is Earc of the Alltraige, a fifth-century figure whose obit may be confused with that of Earc of Slane, who died 512/513 (Chapters 1, 3–6, and *passim*).[56] He is fostered by Íde of Killeedy (d. 570; Chapter 3 and *passim*), and is associated with Fíonán Cam of Kinnitty (d. ca. 600; Chapter 5). He converts Colmán mac Léinín (530–606), founder of Cloyne monastery (Chapter 8), and is given a role directing Iarlaithe mac Loga (d. ca. 540) to the site where Iarlaithe would found Tuam (Chapter 9). On his voyage he has dealings with Éanna of Inishmore, who founded a Christian settlement ca. 490 on the Aran Islands (Chapters 14, 15, 71), and visits a house of Ailbhe of Emly, whose death is given as 527~542 in the annals (Chapter 29). Later, on his return, he visits Brendan of Birr (d. 565 or 572/573; Chapter 94), the British cleric Gildas of Menevia in Wales (d. 567/577; Chapter 83), and travels with Maoineann (d. 572), the first bishop of Clonfert (Chapter 91).[57]

While much of Brendan's chronology is conjectural, the Rawlinson *Vita* appears to embrace the dates given for Brendan's birth and death in the Irish annals. The Rawlinson account asserts that Brendan died in his ninety-third year (Chapter 103), which accords with the Annals of Inisfallen dates of ca. 486 and 578. In Rawlinson, toward the end of his seven-year quest for the *terra repromissionis sanctorum*, he meets the hermit Paul sixty years after St Patrick's death (Chapter 62). Assuming Patrick died in 461, one of two dates given in the Irish annals for Patrick's obit, that would imply a date of 521, when Brendan would have been about thirty-five years old. That same account has Brendan setting out on his voyage soon after being made a priest (Chapter 11), likely by the time he was thirty.[58] Implicitly, then, Rawlinson presents Brendan's *Navigatio* as taking place ca. 515 to ca. 521, when Brendan would have been about twenty-nine to thirty-five years old, and the composition of the *Oratio* ca. 521 at the end of his travels. Rawlinson has Brendan founding Clonfert at age seventy-seven (Chapter 91), implying a date of ca. 563, and well within the range of the dates of 558 and 564 given by the annals.

56. Ó Riain, *Dictionary*, 284–285.

57. Annalistic entries for these saints: Patrick, *AU* 44–45, 46–47, 56–57. Brigit, *AU* 44–45, 66–67; *AI* 58–59, 68–69. Columba, *AI* 66–67, 80–81; *AU* 64–65, 96–97, 98–99. Earc of Slane, *AI* 66–67; *AU* 62–63. Íde, *AI* 74–75; *AU* 84–85. Colmán, *AI* 68–69, 82–83. Ailbhe, *AI* 68–69; *AU* 66–67, 70–71, 72–73. Brendan of Birr, *AU* 84–85, 86–87; *AI* 76–77. Gildas, *AI* 74–75; *AU* 84–85, 88–89. Maoineann, *AU* 86–87.

58. Bede, in his *Ecclesiastical History of the English People*, ca. 731, relates that he was made priest in his thirtieth year. *Bede's Ecclesiastical History of the English People*, ed. Bertram Colgrave and R.A.B. Mynors (Oxford, 1969), 566–567 [V, 24]. Had Rawlinson placed Patrick's death at 493, the alternative date, Brendan would have been about sixty-seven.

Narrative Structure

The Rawlinson *Vita Sancti Brendani* has been faulted, with some justification, for flaws of structure, omission, and narrative confusion. In combining the *Vita* and *Navigatio* traditions, the author, famously, has Brendan reach the *terra repromissionis* at Chapter 65, then return to Ireland at 71, where he relaunches his voyage. "The conflation is crudely done," Plummer observed.[59] He also disparaged the separate voyages as a "gross contradiction."[60] James F. Kenney criticized the "clumsiness of the amalgamation," describing the text as "a very crude conflation of VB [*Vita Brendani*] with NB [*Navigatio Brendani*], consisting simply of the insertion of almost the whole of NB into VB."[61]

Notwithstanding the awkwardness, the author may have conceived of sections of the voyage after Brendan reaches the promised land at 65, but before he is back in Ireland at 77, as *retrospective* elements of the narrative, that is, as tales told after the conclusion of an initial quest. The retrospective element would begin at 67, after Brendan has revisited Ternoc's community, which opens on a reminiscent note: "Among other things, he [Brendan] recounted these as well to them," and would carry through to 76, rounding out the voyage. Plummer himself called attention to this retrospective aspect. "One or two additional incidents of the great voyage are given in the shape of stories told by Brendan to his monks after his return."[62] Even so, the transition is less than seamless.

Rawlinson also lacks the episode in the common version of the *Navigatio* in which Brendan encounters Judas on a rock in the sea, which would have come after 59 and before 60; this story is recounted in retrospective fashion at 97. Finally, Rawlinson at times confuses narrative voice. At 75, the sentence "And what can I say about the old man?" involves an abrupt shift from third person to first before reverting to third again. Similarly, at 100, in the sentence "'Colmán the monk,' he replied to him," the narrative slips from Brendan's first-person account to third person, then back to first again.

Nevertheless, the Rawlinson account bears evidence of planning. Conceived as a triptych, the first part, based on the *Vita* tradition, depicts Brendan's youth; the second part draws on both the *Navigatio* and the *Vita*; the third part makes use of the *Vita* to recount his later life and missions. Within

---

59. *VSH* 1: xxxvii.
60. *LIS* 1: xxi, n1.
61. Kenney, *Sources*, 413.
62. *LIS* 1: xvii. Strijbosch, *Seafaring Saint*, 281, too, noted several "*vita* voyage adventures which Brendan, reminiscing, tells his monks." And Orlandi and Guglielmetti, *Navigatio* (2017), 121, identified "un racconto da parte di Brendano delle meraviglie viste in mare."

this basic pattern, the author faced a challenge in arranging the *Vita's* many discrete elements into a coherent narrative. With the tightly structured *Navigatio* exemplar at hand, indeed effectively defining the broad shape of the story, the author appears to have conceived of each of the two looser *Vita* sections as three thematic groupings that complement each other. The Rawlinson version can thus be approached as a chiastic or ring structure on the following model.

Vita	A. Brendan's birth. (Chapters 1–3)
	B. His youthful sanctity and acts of conversion in Ireland. (4–8)
	C. His early monastic activity in Ireland. (9–12)
Navigatio	D. Barinthus' tale of the *terra repromissionis sanctorum*. (13)
	E. First year at sea. First monk dies; is saved. (14–35)
	E¹. Second year. Second monk attains earthly bliss. (36–54)
	E². Third through sixth years. Third monk dies; is doomed. (55–62)
	D¹. Seventh year. They reach *terra repromissionis*, reminisce. (63–76)
Vita	C¹. Brendan's later monastic activity abroad. (77–87)
	B¹. Acts of deliverance, largely in Ireland. (88–101)
	A¹. Brendan's death. (102–105)

Parsing the Rawlinson account this way may seem mechanical, even contrived. However, as Thomas Owen Clancy has noted, "Medieval Irish writers were fond of a certain chiasmus in their texts, often involving a shaded parallelism or opposition of characters or events." The early Irish travel tale *Immram Máel Dúin*, the Voyage of Máel Dúin, eighth or ninth century, is notable for "the neat structure of its framing episodes."[63] Educated medieval writers and their audiences anticipated and welcomed displays of formal patterning, or *dispositio*, in literary works, sermons, and other compositions that would enlist symmetry and other devices to delight the reader or listener, lend thematic coherency, and exercise the memory.[64]

---

63. Thomas Owen Clancy, "Subversion at Sea: Structure, Style and Intent in the *Immrama*," in *Otherworld Voyage*, ed. Wooding, 194–225, at 206–207.

64. The technique was employed by both religious and secular writers. Matthew's gospel opening is framed as a chiasm: Mt. 1:1–17 cites the names of Christ and his ancestors King David and Abraham, then traces Christ's lineage through three lists of fourteen generations each, and closes by reversing the names Abraham, David, and Christ. The *New Jerome Biblical Commentary*, ed. Raymond E. Brown et al. (Englewood Cliffs, NJ, 1990), 634. The fourteenth-century English alliterative romance *Sir Gawain and the Green Knight* has long been known for its "almost geometrical patterning of persons and events." *Pearl, Cleanness, Patience,*

Commenting on the *Betha Adamnáin* (*Life of Adamnán*), John Carey observed that Adamnán's encounters with a series of unearthly beings form "a tightly interrelated group, conveying a specific message" that promotes his status as an orthodox Christian figure.[65] The encounters are presented in a "ring structure" of ABCB¹A¹ type, and the narrative was "composed with careful, not to say obsessive, attention to thematic coherence and internal symmetry."[66] Writing of the *Navigatio*, O'Meara has noted its "epic repetition and symmetry," and its consciously rhetorical style.[67] It should hardly be surprising that the author of the Rawlinson *Vita*, working in a sophisticated Anglo-Irish literary milieu in an era when authors fully recognized the need to provide "meaning and coherence to amorphous matter" might pay conscious attention to arrangement.[68] If so, the narrative may support analysis on these lines:

In the A/A¹ sequences, Brendan's birth is naturally framed by his saintly death, both featuring common *topoi* involving prophesy, angels, and marvels. In the B/B¹ sequences, Brendan's youthful sanctity and early acts of evangelism in Ireland are played off against his activities in old age, again mostly in Ireland, emphasizing his role in both the advent of the new religion and its salvific effects. In the C/C¹ sequences, Brendan's role as an evangelizer in Ireland is counterposed by his later missions abroad to Britain and the wider Celtic world. In the D/D¹ sequences, which frame the *Navigatio*, Brendan's yearning for, and glimpse of, the *terra repromissionis* prior to setting out on his voyage is followed by his arrival there in the final, seventh year of his travels, and the recounting of

---

Sir Gawain and the Green Knight, ed. A.C. Cawley and J.J. Anderson (London, 1962; repr. 1976), xxiii. It can be approached as an ABC DD¹D² C¹B¹A¹ schema in which a prologue and epilogue comprise the A elements, scenes at Camelot the B elements, Gawain's quest for the Green Chapel and his encounter there with the Green Knight the C elements, and the three central hunting scenes at Bertilak's castle the D elements. Similarly complex patterning is deployed by the English preacher Thomas Wimbledon in his highly regarded fourteenth-century homily *Redde rationem villicationis tuae* (Render an account of thy stewardship). Ione Kemp Knight noted that the sermon is of "the modern or textual" variety which "followed a systematic method of analytical organization." *Wimbledon's Sermon Redde rationem villicationis tue* (Pittsburgh, 1967), 45–46, 48–51. Wimbledon's own commentary throughout the sermon speaks to its complex structure. It can be approached as an A BB¹B² / CC¹C² A¹ schema in which A sets the theme, B represents questions Wimbledon puts to the three estates, C represents by which means, by whom, and on what faults people will be judged, and A¹ concludes the homily.

65. John Carey, "Varieties of Supernatural Contact in the Life of Adamnán," in *Studies in Irish Hagiography: Saints and Scholars*, ed. John Carey et al. (Dublin, 2001), 49–62, at 49.

66. Carey, "Varieties," 59, 61.

67. O'Meara, *Voyage*, xvi–xvii.

68. Eugène Vinaver, *The Rise of Romance* (Oxford, 1971), 68.

additional incidents at sea, drawn from the *Vita* tradition, including the tale of the relaunch.

The three central E/E¹/E² sequences of the *Navigatio*, which comprise the greater part of the traditional voyage tale, relate the story of Brendan's progress through the ecclesiastical calendar, and the tale of three late-coming monks. These sequences also focus on the Mass, monastic discipline, and God's providential care. They feature marvellous elements such as the enigmatic Steward and his heaven-sent provisions, encounters with Satan and his cohorts, Easters spent on the back of Casconius, the vast sea beast, fallen angels in the form of psalm-singing birds, the silent retreat and divinely lit lamps of Ailbhe's community, the Isle of Steadfast Men with its three choirs, rescue from attack by a gryphon and other monstrous beasts, a mysterious crystal column that towers above the sea, an encounter with a disciple of St Patrick, and, ultimately, their visit to the glorious Land of Promise. All these wonders contribute to the *Navigatio*'s enduring fame.

Section E, the first year, sets the seasonal stage for the rest of the voyage. Brendan arrives at the island of the Steward, where one of the monks steals a bridle, repents, dies, and gains heaven. They spend Easter on Casconius and the Easter octave on the Paradise of Birds. After Pentecost, they sail for eight months until they reach Ailbhe's isle, where they spend Christmas and Epiphany, and the first year is complete.

Section E¹, effectively the structural heart of the story, enlists their second year at sea to depict their visit to the idealized monastic community of the Steadfast Men, where the second of the late-coming monks is privileged to stay. While Brendan is in search of the Eden-like Promised Land of the Saints, the monks of the Isle of Steadfast Men live a paradise-like life in closer reach. This core episode depicting monastic life with its focus on Mass and the psalter and its recurring cyclical celebrations as a heaven of sorts on earth is bracketed by stories of God provisioning the monks and delivering them from perils.

Section E² focuses on their middle years at sea, years three through six. It opens with Brendan saying Mass while marine creatures show reverence. They encounter the crystal column where they find a chalice and paten. And they sail to the gates of hell where demons claim the third monk. This section ends with the hermit Paul announcing that they have been six years on their journey and will spend a seventh, final Easter on Casconius, then reach the promised land.

Faced with the task of bringing a measure of coherence to the elements of the rather loose *Vita* tradition to complement the *Navigatio*, the author of the Rawlinson account was not entirely successful in conflating the two. Yet however imperfect, the finished product bears evidence of artistic effort and intentional shaping.

Themes

Presenting Brendan's story in its most developed stage in Latin, and reworking material that predated the Anglo-Norman arrival, the Rawlinson *Vita* goes further than the Dublin and Salamanca versions of his story in glorifying its subject, likening Brendan to Moses (Chapter 5), Abraham (12), and Peter the Apostle (83). It is also rich in additional political, social, and religious material that would have been of interest to its monastic creators, their princely patrons, and their audiences. Medieval clerics made use of memorialization, including history and hagiography, "to explore sticky ethical, political, and metaphysical problems," Thomas O'Donnell has observed, and to reimagine "current political configurations in the elevated terms of the past."[69]

Rawlinson portrays Brendan as a saint of the western Irish, as a peacemaker, and as a patron of the disenfranchised and the afflicted. His activities reflect medieval monastic claims, contemporary Christian doctrine, and clerical discipline. In developing these multiple themes, Brendan's memorializers placed him in an extended world of marvels and encounters that are not found, or are not found so extensively, in the Dublin and Salamanca versions. These marvels speak to the imaginative vitality of Irish culture, encompassing visions, miraculous transformations, resurrections, rescues, cures, angelic interventions, monstrous beasts, and more.

Brendan, Diarmait, and Áed. In depicting Brendan's dealings with Diarmait mac Cerbaill (Chapter 95) and Áed mac Echach (88), the Rawlinson *Vita* foregrounds and exalts its subject to a greater extent than the earlier Dublin *Vita* and other versions. Diarmait mac Cerbaill, a southern Uí Néill king (r. ca. 544 to 565), has "some title to be ranked as the first Christian high-king of Ireland."[70] In 558–560, he was the last pagan ruler to celebrate "the Feast of Temair," thereby claiming to hold the sacral high kingship.[71] Adomnán in his *Life of Columba* (I, 36) says Diarmait was "ordained by God's will as king of all Ireland."[72] In the Rawlinson *Vita* (95), the king has a dream charged with symbolism in which angels remove the golden chain from his neck, and hand it to the saint. When Brendan arrives the next day, "Your kingdom, O king, is at an end," his sages tell him, interpreting his dream. "And this indeed is the one to whom your kingdom is given by God and his angels." In the Dublin account, Brendan, while celebrated, is afforded no comparable exclusivity; he is described as one "among the saints" of Ireland (*Dublin-*

69. Thomas O'Donnell, "Monastic History and Memory," in *Medieval Historical Writing: Britain and Ireland, 500–1500*, ed. Jennifer Jahner et al. (Cambridge, 2019), 35–50, at 50.
70. Francis J. Byrne, *Irish Kings and High-Kings* (Dublin, 2004), 104.
71. *AI* 72–73. *AU* 80–81.
72. *Life of St Columba*, trans. Sharpe, 138.

iensis, M 117) who will inherit authority. Moreover, Rawlinson does not echo Dublin in eulogizing Diarmait as "a staunchly just Catholic king"; rather, it closes with Brendan's stern injunctions to revere God and seek his kingdom, an implicit caution against backsliding. Brendan's association with a king of Tara elevates him as a saint of the Gaelic west, as Patrick's association with the kingship of Tara advanced the claim that he was the metropolitan bishop of all Ireland.[73]

Diarmait's reign as a Christian king was short lived, however. He was defeated by a Connacht king, Áed mac Echach, at Cúl Dreimne in 561.[74] The annals for 578 memorialize Áed mac Echach and note that he granted Enach Dúin (Annagh-down) to Brendan, where his sister Brígh lived (Chapter 102).[75] In Rawlinson, Áed is credited, as well, with giving Inchiquin island to Brendan (88). By linking Brendan to the Áed mac Echach of the Uí Briúin Aí, from whom the latter-day patrons of Brendan's foundations, the Ua Conchobair [O'Connors], traced their descent, Rawlinson associates Brendan with the forerunners of Connacht nobility of the compiler's day, validating the Ua Conchobair dynasty and implying that, like Diarmait, they are worthy of the mantle of the Irish high kingship, sanctified by Brendan, and passed down through the ages.[76]

Brendan and Gildas. By the time Brendan meets Diarmait, his high status as an Irish saint already has been asserted in his encounter with Gildas (ca. 500–570), a saint with British affiliations who has the temerity to put Brendan and his company to the test (Chapters 83–85). In Rawlinson touches that are absent from the Dublin version, Brendan travels to Britain less as a craven penitent following the death of the drowned youth and more as a spirited evangelist on a mission to "teach others and gain souls for Christ." The Holy Spirit reveals to Gildas that "a very great" abbot is about to visit him. Upon Brendan's arrival, snow doesn't settle on him and his company, and fettered gates burst open at his word. At Mass, Brendan's miracles astonish the congregation. He reads a Greek text as readily as if it were Latin, and a terrified Gildas, seeing a human finger on the paten, fears God's judgment for putting Brendan to the test until the saint assures him that "My hand will shield your head from vengeance." Gildas is made to acknowledge that he, a British cleric, is not a fit judge for his Irish counterpart. Ultimately, he begs Brendan to accept him as his "disciple and obedient monk," and to stay and rule over the place, an offer Brendan refuses.

---

73. Michael W. Herren, "Patrick, Gaul, and Gildas: A New Lens on the Apostle of Ireland's Career," in *Gablánach in Scélaigecht*, ed. Sheehan et al., 9–25, at 10.

74. In 565, Diarmait was slain by the Cruthin over-king of Ulster, Áed Dub mac Suibni. Byrne, *Irish Kings*, 95.

75. *AI* 76–77.

76. For more on the relationship between the Ua Conchobair and Brendan's foundations, see Appendix 3.

This episode, fraught with complexity, ambivalence, and tension, serves to assert the worth of Irish clergy in the context of friction between the Anglo-Norman and Irish churches that had been building since the invasion. By the fourteenth century, when the Rawlinson *Vita* is generally thought to have been written, Ireland had become an "ethnically polarized world" of two nations.[77] Brendan's protracted encounter with Gildas evinces that distrust and tension. The Rawlinson author is at pains to emphasize Brendan's dignity and merit as an Irish cleric. His sanctity and learning are exemplary. Triumphing over trials set by the presumptuous Briton, he is shown to be fit to rule a British community but scorns that preferment. Ultimately, only God, not a Briton, is deemed worthy to judge the Irish abbot. The entire episode is a forceful affirmation of Brendan's resilience amid trials, of Irish religious orthodoxy and learning, and of Irish clerical worth in the face of British provocation. The encounter ends with Gildas bowing to Brendan's superiority, a scene that seems calculated to discomfit denigrators of the Irish church.

Brendan as peacemaker. Late in the Rawlinson account, as befits a saint and patron of the west, Brendan is portrayed as a peacemaker who suppresses fighting between Munster and Connacht (101), areas where Gaelic culture held its own in a chaotic era of political upheaval and social conflict. Much earlier, as a youth, he saves a man by causing his assailants to mistake him for a standing stone (6). This repudiation of violence among the native Irish, while a common hagiographic *topos*, would have resonated among those who were exhausted by conflict. In a related vein, the tale of the man from Corcumroe condemns familial discord because "the Lord Jesus Christ is driven away from people by discord, and then the demons draw near" (98). The message may have seemed especially apt for Gaelic communities riven and weakened by rivalry. The central action of the *Navigatio*, Brendan's search for an elusive terrestrial paradise, would also have appealed to those who dreamt of escape from violent, uncertain times. Late in his voyage God directs him to "a very good and holy land undefiled by human blood nor dug up for any man's grave" (76), an imagined landscape to the west, far more appealing than the harsh realities of the day.

Brendan as a patron of the suffering. In a manner reminiscent of Brigidine hagiography, Brendan shuns worldly honours (11, 85), is disdainful of power and wealth, and is identified as a patron and liberator of the poor, the afflicted, and the oppressed. In multiple deliverances, he redeems a monk named Colmán from purgatory (100), frees a man from bondage (90), repeatedly raises the dead

77. Robin Frame, "Ireland after 1169: Barriers to Acculturation on an 'English' Edge," in *Norman Expansion: Connections, Continuities and Contrasts*, ed. Keith J. Stringer and Andrew Jotischky (Farnham, Surrey, 2013), 115–141, at 118.

(11, 67, 68, 89, 91), cures a man mute from birth (101), liberates a settlement from a plague of fleas (79), and saves Gildas' community from lions (85).

Brendan's humanity, and clerical shortcomings. Even as Rawlinson affirms Brendan's sanctity and merit, it lends a touch of verisimilitude by investing him with human frailties, albeit ones that ultimately reflect credit on him. Bishop Earc upbraids him for chastising the Irish maiden who had attempted to seduce him (5). When Brendan asks to remain on Ailbhe's island, the abbot chides him for misreading God's will (33). He needs Íde's counsel to relaunch his voyage (71). He is seized with a pang of conscience for a drowned youth (82). When a beleaguered sea beast invokes Brigit's name for help, not his, Brendan appears to feel resentment or envy (86).

The shortcomings and vices of Irish clerics also are portrayed, in a more critical light. Two of the three late-coming monks in the *Navigatio* sin by stealing a silver-set bridle (19) and by displaying obduracy (15, 59), grave faults in a community pledged to poverty and obedience. There are instances, on Casconius and elsewhere, where the monks are faint of heart (24). A monk cuts down another with a hatchet (89). Another is self-righteous during a visit to Brendan of Birr and refuses to eat the food provided (94). The monks can be complainers (97), and as the monk Colmán acknowledges, they can be wrathful and unruly (100).

Monastic claims, Christian dogma, and clerical discipline. The Rawlinson account associates Brendan's houses with regal patrons of the stature of Diarmait (95) and Áed (88), and by implication their princely successors in the author's own era, to affirm and defend monastic privileges, and to attract donors and pilgrims, all pertinent issues. In a clear act of royal patronage, Áed grants Brendan land on Inchiquin Island (88). Presented with gold that Brendan has dug up to ransom a man from bondage, a king declares that "Christ's gold is not mine to keep but belongs to his servants," deferring to ecclesiastical privilege (90). When Brendan dies, the monk carrying his body to Clonfert for burial encounters Curryn mac Setni, who threatens to waylay the body; after offering Curryn gold, the monk promises that he will rise above his brothers to rule the locale, provided he associates himself with Brendan by allowing the body to proceed to Clonfert (102), an allusion to the value of relics throughout the Middle Ages.[78]

Additionally, the narrative reflects contemporary Christian issues and attests to the Irish church's orthodoxy. Gildas has a grisly glimpse at Mass of Christ's body in the form of a finger on the paten and blood in the chalice (84), affirming the doctrine of the "real presence," defined as "transubstantiation" by the

78. In the *Second Irish Life, Brussels*, 207, Curryn is promised not only gold and kingship but also heaven before he relents. *LIS* 1: 94 (Irish); 2: 91–92 (English).

Fourth Lateran Council in 1215. And when Brendan is presented with a Greek text, he says, "Christ, let your writings be open to us," affirming his authority and implying that the Christian message is open to all, irrespective of nation or language. Brendan redeems the monk Colmán's soul through prayer (100), a doctrine promoted by the Second Council of Lyons in 1274. His vision of "most grievous heresy" in Britain (87), while opaque, subtly deflates English claims to orthodox exclusivity or superiority, even as it reflects the anxiety that haunted ecclesiastical and secular authorities in the twelfth and thirteenth centuries in the face of dissenting sects and beliefs.[79]

Finally, the story alludes to monastic and church discipline, perennial issues. Brendan's monks eat salt pork without sinning on Good Friday, a day of abstinence (94), because holy scripture and the brotherly rule enjoin them to humbly eat what is set before them. The tale of the man from Corcumroe and his two wives, "according to the law at that time," carries a reminder that the church reforms of the twelfth and thirteenth centuries firmly rejected the Irish custom of secondary wives (98).

Marvels and miracles. As a hagiographer, the author of the Rawlinson *Vita* spared no effort in depicting Brendan's sanctity, unwavering trust in providence, acts of power, prophetic insight, and marvellous encounters. Marvels are attributed to him before his birth (1). In his youth he is attended by angels (3), he prophesies (9), raises the dead (11 and *passim*), and saves a man from enemies by making him appear to be a standing stone (6). Later, he presides over miracles at Mass (84), faces down pagan kings and their seers (88, 95), redeems a soul after death (100), averts war among his fellow Gaels (101), tames lions (85), ransoms slaves (90), and scorns worldly preferment (11, 85). During his voyage in search of the Promised Land of the Saints, a terrestrial paradise, he celebrates Easter on the back of a great sea beast (24, 39), catches a glimpse of Satan and hell (67), meets Judas on a rock in the sea (97), evades demons (59, 70), meets fellow monks who live angelic lives on remote islands (29–35, 47–50), and finally attains this promised land (65).

A notable difference between the *Vita* and *Navigatio* traditions is that in the former, Brendan actively performs the miracles one would expect of a

---

79. While popular heresy gained little foothold in England during this period, it flourished on the Continent after 1150, where it was fiercely repressed. In 1184, Pope Lucius III and the Holy Roman Emperor Frederick Barbarossa "jointly condemned and proscribed the sects of Cathars, Patarines, Humiliati, Poor of Lyons, Passagians, Josephini, and Arnoldists," and the Fourth Lateran Council in 1215 spelled out procedures for suppressing heretics and their supporters. Walter L. Wakefield and Austin P. Evans, trans., *Heresies of the High Middle Ages* (New York, London, 1969), 28, 33. On the Albigenses/Cathars and the Waldenses, Pietro Parente et al., *Dictionary of Dogmatic Theology*, trans. Emmanuel Doronzo (Westminster, MD, 1974), 5–6, 298.

saint, while in the latter, marvels attend him, but he does not perform them himself.[80]

Style

Like the Rawlinson manuscript itself, the Latin of the Rawlinson *Vita* is not heavily adorned. However, its stylistic features exalt its protagonist, colour important scenes, and vary the tone. These features can be evocative, shocking, playful, and raw.

The opening words liken Brendan to an *aurora rutilans*, a "shining dawn" that drives away the *peccatorum tenebras*, "the darkness of sin," and playfully say that the famous mariner provides a *portum salutis*, a "harbour of salvation," for those adrift on a sea of vice (Chapter 1). When Satan casts a spell on a young girl to attempt to seduce Brendan (5), Brendan's psalm chanting, *caneret*, contrasts with the devil's enchantments, *incantavit*. Brendan is likened to *mons Syon*, Mount Sion, when in his rock-like faith (6) he rescues a man from enemies by disguising him as a standing stone, and there is Latin wordplay on committing oneself to the rock of Christ, and on how the man seems to be a rock and a rock a man. The water Brendan causes to flow from the earth (7) is described as *aquas vivas*, running water, but also with a spiritual sense of living water. When he converts Colmán mac Léinín (8), Brendan dubs him *Colmanum, quasi columbe manum* (dove-hand) in recognition of his newfound innocence. He similarly plays on words when he meets Paul the hermit, who is clad only in his own hair (61), saying that although he himself wears a *habitum monachi*, a monk's habit, he does not do anything worthy of the habit he wears, *non facio actum dignum habitui*.

When Brendan encounters Satan (67), the devil announces that *in obscuris enim maris locis mansiones pessimas habemus*, "we make our wretched dwellings in the secret places of the sea," evoking a dark, demonic world that contrasts with the luminous paradise they have been seeking where "Christ himself is the light" (13). When the brothers find a spring from which they hope to drink (70), they bless it and see a *diabolum immundos liquores effundentem*, a demon spewing foul fluids, a revolting image, and abruptly lose their craving.

Gildas' vision at Mass (84), where he sees a *digitum humanum in disco, et sanguinem in calice*, a human finger on the paten and blood in the chalice, is grotesquely orthodox but makes the point. In another grotesque incident, a self-important monk who spurns the brotherly rule to eat what is placed before him (94) and eats bread rather than the meat he is offered on Good Friday, is treated to a grisly sight the next day: *residuum conversi de suo pane cruda caro scaturiens*

---

80. Mackley, *Legend*, 19.

vermes apparebat, the remains of his bread appeared to be raw flesh, swarming with worms.

Finally, Brendan's death (103) is conveyed in a rhythmic syntax, with verbal echoes and contrasts, that lifts the saint amid angelic exultation from the arms of his grieving community into paradise, pairing such words as *terra* and *coelum*, *discipulus* and *angelus*, to emphasize his translation. *Et tunc, his dictis verbis, inter manus sanctorum discipulorum suorum, expletis nonaginta tribus annis, perfectus Christi imitator existens, angelis quorum disciplinam tenuit in terris exultantibus, migravit ad celum.* "And then, having uttered these words in the hands of his holy disciples, the proven perfect imitator of Christ departed to heaven at the age of ninety-three, as the angels whose teaching he kept on earth rejoiced."

The *Oratio Sancti Brendani*

The *Oratio Sancti Brendani* is an Irish *lorica*, a prayer for protection and deliverance attributed to Brendan, who is said to have composed a version of it at sea. The text offered here is translated from Pierre Salmon's edition based on Munich, Bayerische Staatsbibliothek, Clm 13067, fols. 9r–16v, one of twenty-five Latin manuscripts as well as ten translations into Italian, French, and English he identified.[81] The manuscript, "clearly insular" in decoration, and written ca. 1075, originated in the scriptorium of Waulsort Abbey, a Benedictine *monasterium peregrinorum* in Belgium founded by Irish monks ca. 945.[82] Written in two hands, the script is a Caroline miniscule influenced by the diplomatic hand of the Liège diocese.[83] The manuscript, on 231 vellum folios of 27 cm by 18.5 cm, is rubricated throughout, with large, decorated capitals, and marginal decoration, and has full-page colour depictions of the Virgin and Christ enthroned, receiving a child into the monastery; the descent of Christ from the cross with an Anglo-Saxon runic inscription that transcribes the Latin phrase *Jhesus Nazarenus Rex Iudæorum*; King David with the harp; and Christ

---

81. Pierre Salmon, ed., *"Oratio sancti Brendani,"* in *Testimonia Orationis Christianæ Antiquioris, Corpus Christianorum Continuatio Mediaevalis* 47 (Turnhout, 1977), xxii–xxiii.

82. Carl Selmer, "The Runic Inscription of *Codex Latinus Monacensis* 13067," *Publications of the Modern Languages Association* 53, no. 3 (1938): 645–655, at 654. And Georges Despy, "Le scriptorium de l'abbaye de Waulsort au XIe siècle: La provenance du psautier-hymnaire Munich, Bayer. Staatsbibl. Clm. 13067," *Le Moyen Age* 59 (1953): 87–115, at 91. "L'influence insulaire, visible dans le contenu liturgique du psautier, est pleinement perceptible par l'esprit de la décoration et la technique d'ornementation d'une partie des enluminures." Despy, "Scriptorium," 104.

83. Despy, "Scriptorium," 106.

in glory.[84] It contains a psalter, with additions introduced at Waulsort and at its dependency at Hastière-par-delà. They include a calendar, tables of computus for dating Easter, prayers to the Virgin, the *Oratio Brendani*, prefaces to the psalter (including a Greek alphabet), glosses to the psalter, and prayers, canticles, litanies, offices, and hymns. St Brigit, St Patrick, and St Faolán, possibly Brendan's brother, are included in the calendar as well as in the litany of saints.[85]

The *lorica* genre has been described by Louis Gougaud as a chiefly defensive prayer in litany form, commonly prolix, written either in Latin or a Celtic language such as Irish, in which a petitioner urgently implores the protection of the Trinity, angels, and saints, against attack by the devil and other spiritual or material dangers and harms. The petitioner begs God and his hosts to serve as a defensive shield, a *lorica* in Latin and "lúirech" in Irish, a metal breastplate or leather cuirass. Biblical sources, including Isaiah 59:17 with its reference to the Lord putting on "justice as a breastplate [*lorica*]," appear to have provided inspiration for the *lorica* tradition. St Paul, writing to the Ephesians and Thessalonians, invoked the "breastplate of justice" [Eph. 6:14] and the "breastplate of faith and charity" [1 Thess. 5:8], and urged them to put on "the armour of God, that you may be able to stand against the deceits of the devil" [Eph. 6:11]. Typically, it was chanted, as the *Oratio* is meant to be, and Gougaud noted that some share the characteristics of magical incantations or charms.[86]

The *Faeth Fiada* prayer, or *Patrick's Breastplate*, most likely composed in the eighth century, calls itself "a breastplate of faith, to protect body and soul against

---

84. Selmer, "Runic Inscription," 655. Salmon, *Oratio*, xxvii–xxviii. "Munich, Bayerische Staatsbibliothek, MS Clm 13067, *Psalter of Hastières/Waulsort*. Latin, s. xi/xii, distinct manuscript, Continental manuscripts, vellum," CODECS: Collaborative Online Database and e-Resources for Celtic Studies https://codecs.vanhamel.nl/Munich,_Bayerische_Staatsbibliothek,_MS_Clm_13067. Accessed 20 May 2023.

85. The *Book of Uí Maine*, late fourteenth century, and a Laud Misc. 610 record, fifteenth century, give Brendan three brothers: "Domaingein uil a Tuaim Muscraide et Faichlech Chluana Tuaiscirt et Faelan Chilli Tulach." Ó Riain, *Corpus Genealogiarum*, 59 item 384, whom Ó Riain identified as Domhainghin of Toomyvara in present day Tipperary, and Faithleach of Cloontuskert and Faolán of Kiltullagh, both in Roscommon, Galway. The St "Foillan" in the calendar for October 31, on fol. 3v, with several saints with Irish associations, is likely to be Brendan's brother St Faolán of Kiltullagh or St Faolán of Aachen, himself associated with Connacht. Ó Riain, *Dictionary*, 115, 303–304. Among those also listed for the same date are St Quintin, namely Cobhthach Caol of Drumbo in County Down, Ulster, and St Rumold, a bishop of Dublin. For Quintin, see Ó Riain, *Dictionary*, 177; for Rumold, see *Martyrologium Romanum*, June 24, "Mechliniae, in Brabantia, passio sancti Rumoldi, Episcopi Dublinensis et Martyris, e Scotorum Rege progeniti." *Martyrologium Romanum: Gregorii papae XIII iussu editum, Urbani VIII et Clementis X auctoritate recogniti, ac deinde anno MDCCXLIX Benedicti XIV opera ac studio emendatum et auctum* (Rome, 1948), 149.

86. Louis Gougaud, "Étude sur les *loricae* celtiques et sur les prières qui s'en rapprochent," *Bulletin d'ancienne littérature et d'archéologie chrétiennes* 2 (1912): 115.

demons and men and vices."[87] The *Faeth Fiada* in relatively brief space invokes the Trinity, Christ's redemptive actions, the angels, biblical figures, the powers of nature and humanized attributes of God as a defence against evil powers, false religion, and physical harm. Brendan's *Oratio* is a much more elaborate exercise. Long regarded as a particularly lengthy *lorica*, it draws on multiple sources including the Christian *Litany of the Saints* tradition, biblical deliverances, the Latin/Irish *lorica* tradition, arcana, the *Confiteor* prayer acknowledging sinfulness, and other prayers.

Salmon presented the *Oratio* in three parts comprising twelve sections. Part I contains a profession of faith in God, the heavenly host, and the sacred scriptures; Part II includes the *lorica* proper; and Part III contains a *Confiteor*. Each part features an invocation of the Trinity.

Part I, Section 1, references Brendan's fame as a seafarer and affirms his authorship and his authority as a protector and intercessor, promising that those who say this prayer will have their sins remitted. Section 2 opens with the formula for the Sign of the Cross and presents a litany of Christ's life followed by the formula "spare me." Section 3 is a prayer to the Trinity. Sections 4 through 7 all begin with the formula "deliver me." Section 4 invokes the seven days of creation; Section 5, the nine orders of angels; Section 6 includes a lengthy list of Old Testament deliverances; and Section 7, a somewhat shorter list of New Testament deliverances.

In Part II, Section 8 contains a litany of invocations that functions as an introduction to the *lorica* proper. It opens by invoking the Trinity to remit "all my sins past, present, and soon to be." Section 9 invokes Mary, the nine orders of angels, Michael the Archangel, John the Baptist, the apostles, evangelists, and "all the saints of God" for their prayers and intercession. A second litany asks Mary and the angels to "pray for me," and the "chosen ones of God" to "intercede for me." A third litany of Christ's life follows, with the formula "defend me." A fourth litany lists "all holy disciples of the Lord, and their holy successors," beseeching them to "pray for me." Section 10 is the *lorica*, invoking "these and all the saints, with the perfect Trinity" to "be a breastplate for my soul and spirit and body." The prayer enumerates the petitioner's body parts, and seeks protection in a variety of directions, places, activities, and times. It then invokes God in incantatory fashion under a variety of arcane divine names "qui donnent au morceau un charactère un tant soit peu magique."[88] This, too, is part of a basic *lorica* prayer, although in some manuscripts the list is altered or suppressed entirely. This sec-

87. John Carey, *King of Mysteries: Early Irish Religious Writings* (Dublin, 1998), 129–130. Pierre Salmon contended that the *Oratio*, too, was early and of Irish provenance, provisionally dating it to the eighth century. Salmon, *Oratio*, xxxiv, xxxvi.
88. Salmon, *Oratio*, xxxiii.

tion closes with a petition for protection from a variety of psychological and physical fears and dangers.

In Part III, Section 11 consists of a confession of the seven sins. It invokes the Trinity, renounces the devil and sin, and seeks relief from premature death and eternal torment. Section 12 opens with a *Kyrie*, a Lord's Prayer, and a *Credo*, and a commendation that those for whom the prayer is chanted may enjoy health in this world and salvation in the next.

The *Oratio* is noteworthy for its length. It has multiple Trinitarian invocations, characteristic of its genre. The phrase *Epheta, quod est adaperire*, repeated three times, has an incantatory feel, though it is a phrase used in the gospel, and the baptismal ritual.[89] The prayer seeks the remission of sins past, present, future, and soon to be (*imminentia*). The *lorica* invokes arcane names for God and the use of the psalm tradition that includes a plea for protection from "the arrow that flieth in the day, of the business that walketh about in the dark" [Ps. 90:6].

Salmon drew attention to wording in the *Oratio* and *Navigatio* that he suggested links the two. In the *Oratio*, an invocation reads: *Libera me, Domine, sicut liberasti David de furore ursi et leonis et Goliae et Saulis*, and later, *Libera me, Domine, sicut liberasti Susannam de falsis testibus et Ionam de ventre ceti*.[90] He argued that this language influenced the *Navigatio*. When a monstrous sea beast attacks Brendan and his monks, the *Navigatio* says: *Fratres magis ac magis timebant. Venerabilis quoque senex extensis manibus in caelum dixit: 'Domine, libera servos tuos sicut liberasti David de manu Goliae gigantis! ... Domine, libera nos sicut liberasti Ionam de potestate ceti magni!'*[91] The *Oratio* also refers to Elijah and his deliverance of the widow's dead son with the aside "*quem multi dicunt Ionam esse, iterum de ventri caeti ereptum*" in yet another reference to the biblical story.[92] That said, while the *Oratio* claims to have been composed during Brendan's voyage, its references to the dangers at sea are few and generic.

Perhaps the most extraordinary element in the *Oratio* is the extravagant promises made in its initial rubric: "Truly, I say that whoever shall chant this prayer for himself or for his friend, whether living or dead, his sins will be remitted, and he will be spared future punishments. If this prayer is chanted ten times on bended knees, or prostrate, it has the worth of a hundred readings of the psalter, a hundred Masses and a hundred prayers for the dead." As Salmon notes, the *Oratio* was composed in an age before church liturgies became fixed and

---

89. Salmon, *Oratio*, xxxvi. See Mk. 7:34, where Jesus heals the man who was deaf and mute with the command: "Ephpheta, which is, Be thou opened."

90. Salmon, *Oratio*, ix–x.

91. Orlandi and Guglielmetti, *Navigatio* (2014), 62.

92. Salmon, *Oratio*, 8.

speaks to a spirituality informed by the Bible's record of salvation history.[93] That spirituality, Brendan's fame, and the generous indulgences the *Oratio* promises, ensured its survival in manuscripts in Latin and other languages down to the eve of the modern age.

A Note on the Translation

This translation is based on Plummer's edition of the *Vita Prima Sancti Brendani*, from his *Vitae Sanctorum Hiberniae*, corrected against a digitized photographic copy of the manuscript supplied by the Bodleian Library, and on Salmon's edition of the *Oratio Sancti Brendani*. While faithful to the ecclesiastical Latin of the originals, the translation is not literal; it offers a contemporary, readable interpretation of the originals, with explanatory notes.

Routine honorifics before a saint's name, such as *Sanctus Brandanus, Pater Brandanus, Sanctus Episcopus Ercus*, and the like, are noted on first use, then generally are omitted, as are repetitive allusions to the "holy father," "holy nun," "holy bishop," "holy pastor," and so on. Words such as *quidam* (a certain person, thing), *ecce* (behold), *scilicet* (that is to say, namely), and *praedictus* (the aforesaid, aforementioned), which clutter the original and feel stilted in translation, also often are omitted. Connectives, including "and," "but," "for," "so," may be omitted, and the demonstratives "this" and "that" may be replaced by the articles "a" and "the."

The English title, The *Life of St Brendan*, follows Plummer, as do the chapter divisions. The titles for the sections and the chapters are editorial. Titles for Brendan's *Prayer* also are editorial.

Because of Brendan's fame, the anglicized version of his Irish name, Bréanainn, is used. Similarly, Patrick (Patricius), Columba (Colum Cille) and Brigit (Brighid). Generally, the names of Clonfert and other well-known locales have been anglicized. Elsewhere, the spelling of Irish personal and place names conforms to usage in Pádraig Ó Riain's *Dictionary of Irish Saints*, and in *A New History of Ireland*.[94]

Biblical citations are from the Vulgate Bible, in the Dumbarton Oaks edition of the Douay-Rheims version published by Harvard University Press. Explanatory editorial material is provided within square brackets for Irish names, locales, biblical citations, liturgical times and seasons, and medieval navigation, weights, and measures.

93. Salmon, *Oratio*, xxxiii–xxxiv.

94. T.W. Moody, F.X. Martin, F.J. Byrne, W.E. Vaughan, Art Cosgrove, J.R. Hill, and Dáibhí Ó Cróinín, eds., *A New History of Ireland* (Oxford, 1976–2011), 8: 4–5.

Finally, a close comparison of Plummer's edition and a photocopy of the Rawlinson manuscript yields a few trivial discrepancies and errors. Missing from the edition in Chapter 31 are *per tota tempora* (79v, B4) and *ex eis* (B12); in Chapter 33, MS 80r, A30 has *quo* with superscript, likely for *quomodo*. At Chapter 61, MS has *suis secretis* (84v, B18–19), where *suis* is lacking in the edition. At Chapter 62, *ad huc* is omitted before *usque ad pascha* (85r, B3). Also, at B5–6, MS appears to have *per cepta* where the edition has been emended to *accepta*. At Chapter 75, Plummer finds *inuento* (87r, A37) corrupt and suggests *inueteratus*, but *inuento* (found) is not necessarily unlikely. At Chapter 97, MS has *uobis dicam* (90r, A30) where the edition has *dicam uobis*.

The Life of St Brendan

Brendan's Youth

Brendan's birth. (1) There was a man of venerable life, Brendan by name, who, like the shining dawn, drove the darkness of sin from the hearts of many and offered sure guidance to the harbour of salvation for those gone astray on a sea of vices. He was born among the Ciarraige people.[1] His father, Fionnlugh, was a faithful and wise man.[2] His mother's name was Cara. They both lived chastely in accordance with the precepts of the holy bishop Earc.[3] Indeed, his mother Cara had a dream before the blessed son was born: Her bosom was filled with pure gold, and her breasts shone with a bright light. When the marvellous dream was recounted to Earc, inspired by the [Holy] Spirit, he said to her husband: "Your wife will bear you a son of great power to light the world with the splendour of sanctity." The woman conceived, and in due course gave birth to the promised son.

1. *R* 98 *de Kerraigensium genere;* the Ciarraige people gave their name to Kerry. *M* 103 has Brendan born in the Ciarraige region of Munster near present day Tralee in Kerry. *Lismore* 247 and *Brussels* 44 (all *Brussels* references are to Plummer's *LIS*, 2: 44–92) say he was from Ciarraige Lúachra, the Tralee Bay region, and was born when Óengus mac Nad Froích (d. 490/492) was king of Munster, as do the notes to the *Martyrology of Oengus.* Whitley Stokes, ed., *Félire Óengusso Céli Dé = The Martyrology of Oengus the Culdee* (London, 1905; repr. Dublin, 1984), 132–133.

2. *Lismore* 248 and *Brussels* 44 say Fionnlugh was a freeman or noble of the Alltraige Caille country around Tralee and is presented as a pagan – Brendan later converts him (Chapter 71). *Lismore* 247 adds that he was of the tribe of Ciar, son of Fergus. Commentary on the *Martyrology of Oengus* calls Brendan "Brénaind son of Findlug, son of Elchu, son of Aelta of the Ciarraige Luachra of Alltraige Caille." Stokes, *Martyrology*, 132–133. For an extended pedigree preserved in the genealogical record, see Pádraig Ó Riain, ed., *Corpus Genealogiarum Sanctorum Hiberniae* (Dublin, 1985), 22 item 127.1, 2.

3. Earc of the Alltraige was a fifth-century figure associated with sites near Ardfert, Brendan's foundation. Pádraig Ó Riain, *A Dictionary of Irish Saints* (Dublin, 2012), 284.

A king's fosterage. (2) At that time, a seer, Bec mac Dé, happened to be lodged nearby at the house of a powerful man [Macc Ardae mac Fidaig, king of Ciar-raige Lúachra].[4] When the seer was questioned by the host as to what the future held, he confidently replied: "A child will be born this night by the sea who will be your future lord. He will rule not only over you but also many others."[5] When the rich man heard of that coming lord, the next day at dawn he diligently sought out the place where the boy was born. Finding the precious pearl, like a second Simeon the Just he humbly took him into his arms [Lk. 2:25–35]. And offering a gift to so great a lord, he presented him with thirty cows that had given birth to as many bull calves that same night and said: "I acknowledge you as my foster child, and future lord."

Íde's care. (3) A wondrous sight appeared to confirm the holiness of the new-born child, which Earc witnessed on the night of his birth. For he saw the whole region where the boy was born shine with a great light, and angels in white gar-ments fly in the air. Rising the next day, he came to the place where the boy was born. Taking him in his hands he raised him up, and said: "Man of God, accept me, a monk, as your kinsman. Man of God, let men's hearts be glad and rejoice at your coming, and mine above all." And he prayed to God on bent knee, weep-ing. Then, rising from prayer, the man of God baptized the child, calling him Brendan, for there was a heavy dew on the day of his baptism.[6] Moreover, that earthly dew signified the spiritual dew with which the holy boy's soul was filled, and the sweet heavenly gifts with which it was endowed.

After the blessed child was weaned in his parents' home, Earc took him and entrusted him to the care of the holy virgin Íde [of Killeedy in Limerick].[7] For this

4. Bec mac Dé, whose death *AU* 78–79 records in 553, was the chief prophet for Diair-mait mac Cerbaill (r. 544 to 565), who foretold the end of Diarmait's reign (Chapter 95). For "powerful man," *M* 103 has *filius Airde*. *Lismore* 248 and *Brussels* 45 have Airdi son of Fidach. Macc Ardae mac Fidaig, king of Ciarraige Lúachra, reportedly made an alliance with Brendan and other West Munster saints on behalf of the Ciarraige with the Múscraige and other sur-rounding peoples. Francis J. Byrne, *Irish Kings and High-Kings* (Dublin, 2004), 216. Macc Ardae's reception of the infant Brendan recalls Simeon's reception of Jesus (Lk. 2:25–32), and the Magi's presentation of rich gifts (Mt. 2:9–11).

5. The notes to the *Martyrology* also recount the visions of Brendan's mother and Bishop Earc and the prophesy of Bec mac Dé to Macc Ardae mac Fidaig. Stokes, *Martyrology*, 132–133.

6. *Lismore* 248 and *Brussels* 45 derive Brendan's name from "broen finn" or "braenfind," the white rain or mist that fell on the night he was born. Both say his parents called him Mobhi. The notes to the *Martyrology* say his name is derived from a "broen," a drop that originated in the river Jordan and was "dian" (swift), "di-anuas" (from above), and which fell "denus" (at the time) of his baptism. Stokes, *Martyrology*, 132–133.

7. For Íde (d. 570) see *AI* 74–75; *AU* 84–85. *M* 104 locates Íde at Cluain Credhal/Ceall Yte, Killeedy, near Sliab Luachra/Slieve Lougher in Kerry, east of Tralee in the land of the Uí Chonaill Ghabhra.

virgin fostered from infancy many of the saints of Ireland. One day, when the child had reached the age when he could speak and converse, the nurse, seeing the boy's face bathed with joy, said: "O holy child, what so causes you to smile?" He replied: "Because I see you and others like you, many in number, ever speaking to me, and they gladden me, holding me in their hands."[8]

Earc's instruction. (4) After he was fostered at the virgin's home for five years, and was taught good habits, the bishop took charge of him to teach him to read and write. The boy grew, and waxed strong in the Lord, and through his good habits displayed proofs of holiness. Indeed, the heavenly Teacher [God] who enlightened him inwardly subdued the wild creatures of the woods to his will. For when he was still a boy, and craved milk as children of that age do but had none of the longed-for drink because Earc had no cows, he prayed to God to assist him in his distress, trusting in him who provides food for the ravens' young when they cry to him [Ps. 146:9]. And since the prayer of a just man pierces the heavens, a deer with her fawn, made tame as a sheep, coming daily from a nearby mountain [Slieve Lougher], supplied him with an abundance of milk to meet his needs.[9]

He also had a virgin sister, Brígh, whom he deeply cherished because, while the natural kinship of blood made her dear, the brightness of grace made her dearer still. For when this grace illumined the boy's inner eyes, at times he saw his sister's face resemble the radiant moon, and he beheld the face of his teacher Earc like the sphere of the sun.

Chastising a maiden. (5) When the boy was ten years old, on a day when he once again accompanied the bishop to instruct the people in his charge, they came to the preaching place. Climbing down from the chariot to sow the word of life in his listeners' hearts, the man of God entrusted the chariot and other equipment to his pupil's care. As he [Brendan] devoutly sang psalms to his God, the enemy [Satan], jealous of his good works, bewitched a noble maiden and stirred her to have her way with him.[10] Coming to the chariot, the royal maiden pleaded with the boy Brendan to let her climb into it and have her way with him. Recoiling from the idea, the true lover of chastity immediately ordered her to be gone, lest the woman's depraved suggestions corrupt his soul.[11] When she refused to heed his warnings, reproving her with chiding words, he said: "Why

8. The ancient notion that innocent children can see angels.

9. *M* 105 has *monte Luachra*. *Lismore* 249 and *Brussels* 46 have Sliab Luachra/Slieve Lougher.

10. Cf. 1 Cor. 15:33: "Be not deceived; evil communications corrupt good manners." As well, 1 Cor. 10:7–8 condemns idolaters who "rose up to play," recalling Ex. 32:6, and fornicators.

11. In *M* 106, Brendan does not want to be distracted from reading the divine office.

have you come here, accursed among women?[12] Go back to your people and
have dealings with someone your own age!" When she refused to go back, taking
up a whip he struck her. And because vexation brings understanding [Isa. 28:19],
though sad, she returned, chastened, to her people.

When the homily was over, the bishop, returning to the chariot,
reproached the boy, saying: "Why did you strike a maiden who knows not sin?
Do penance, therefore, for such rashness and fault." The true professor of
humility replied, saying: "I am ready, Father, to do whatever you say. Tell me
what you want, and I will carry it out." When the father heard that the boy was
disposed to obey, he put off for a time the intended penance. As they were
returning home and drew near a cave on the way, the elder said to the pupil:
"Stay in this cave until tomorrow morning." Accordingly, Brendan immediately went into the cave and remained for the time set by the father, contem-
plating the heavens, and praying and singing psalms.[13] His teacher, unbe-
knownst to the pupil, sat close by the place, observing. And like another Jacob,
he saw angels descending and ascending all through the night between the cave
and the sky [Gen. 28:11–12]. From that time, God so greatly adorned St Brendan's countenance with glory that people could not look on his face, as if he
were another Moses, except for holy Fíonán Cam [d. 600, abbot of Kinnitty in
Offaly], who was accorded similar grace.[14]

Saving a man from enemies. (6) Nor should it be overlooked how, at another
time as he accompanied his teacher on a journey, through prayer he saved a fellow traveller, a layman, from onrushing enemies. For as they walked together on
the way, that man's enemies suddenly came upon them. When he had seen
them, seeking refuge in the holy men's protection, he said: "Shelter me under the
shadow of your wings [Ps. 16:8]. For my enemies draw near intending to kill
me." The boy Brendan, as steadfast in faith as Mount Sion, said to him: "Go,
man, to that standing stone by the road, and fear not the presence of enemies.
For God can make sons of men from stones if he wishes" [Mt. 3:9]. Going to the
stone and entrusting himself to Christ the living rock like an invincible shield,
and trusting in the holy men's prayers, the man awaited his fate. What more is
there to say? Like a second Moses on the hill of contemplation, Brendan the
holy youth lifted pure hands in prayer against those Amalechites and sapped
their strength [Ex. 17:9–13]. For he blessed the man and the stone at the same
time, and to the pursuers the stone appeared to be a man, and the man a stone.

12. *Maledicta inter mulieres*, a scathing allusion to Eve, through whom humankind fell
from grace, and a contrast to the Virgin Mary, who is *benedicta in mulieribus*, blessed among
women.

13. *Lismore* 250 adds that Brendan's voice could be heard 1,000 paces away.

14. This is the first time that Brendan is called a saint.

The pursuers' eyes being deceived, they thought they were slaying their foremost enemy, but in fact they were striking the stone next to him. The man of God did this near Irluacair through the power of him who turned Lot's wife into a stone statue [Gen. 19:26].[15] And the stone, struck in this way by the man's enemies, is visible to this day in that very place like a body without a head, as a wonder to many [Ps. 70:7]. Seeing the blindness of their heart and eyes, Earc was moved to pity, and reproving their hardness of heart, he said: "O men, do penance, and see that you were striking a stone and you carried off a part of it, thinking it to be your enemy's head. In fact, he has escaped." Then those men, seven in number, did penance and remained in the service of God under Earc's rule until the day they died.

Drawing water from the earth. (7) Another time when the holy men sat together on a mountain, Sliab Luachra, and the elder nearly fainted from thirst in the summer heat, the pupil, distressed by the teacher's need, commanded the earth, though much parched by the summer drought, to bring forth fresh water through the power of him who brought forth an abundance of water from the hardest rock [Ps. 77:16]. And at his word, the earth immediately brought forth a spring, and to this day running water flows, a witness to Brendan's holiness.[16]

Colmán of Cloyne. (8) After this, the gifted youth Brendan, burning with love for the holy scriptures, and longing to see other models of saintly life, having obtained his teacher's permission, thought first that he would visit holy Iarlaithe the bishop [Iarlaithe mac Loga (d. ca 540), founder of Tuam in Galway], and afterward other godly men of the country. But before he reached Iarlaithe, he went to his nurse Íde seeking her blessing as an inheritance. "Go and learn the rules of the saints who have perfected them," she told him. "Learn not from maidens, lest you be reproached by men" [1 Cor. 14:34–35]. Then, inspired by the Holy Spirit, Íde foretold her foster child that he would encounter a certain layman who would be reckoned among God's saints. As Brendan went on his way, he met a man on the road as his nurse predicted. He was Colmán, son of Léinín. Brendan said to him: "Do penance, man, for God calls you to salvation, and you will be like an innocent dove in the sight of God."[17] Therefore, he named that Colmán *Columbe-manum* [dove-hand] as it were, for the innocence of his

15. R 101 *Luacayr.* Irluacair, a territory in Munster bordering Kerry, Cork, and Limerick. The incident is a possible borrowing from the *Táin Bó Cúailnge*, in which the hero Cethern mac Fintain attacks a pillar-stone, thinking it to be Ailill mac Mátae. Cecile O'Rahilly, ed., *Táin Bó Cúailnge: Recension 1*, 3317–3319 (Dublin, 1976), 100 [Irish], 213 [English]. This connects the *Vita* with an early ninth-century text. O'Rahilly, *Táin Bó*, ix.

16. M 107 adds that the place is known as Brendan's Spring.

17. M 107 adds: "and a glorious column in his temple" (translations are mine unless otherwise indicated).

deeds.[18] This Colmán son of Léinín was distinguished among the saints for his life and teaching. For he founded Cloyne church, which today is a cathedral church, and renowned in the region of Munster.

Visiting Iarlaithe. (9) After this Brendan came to Iarlaithe, who lived in Connacht at the time. Staying with the holy man for a while, he continued to thirstily drink in draughts of saving doctrine.[19] And he also began to grow strong in the spirit of prophesy, among other gifts of God. For at one time, inspired by the Spirit, he made known to Iarlaithe where he would be buried, in this way: "Not here will you rise again, father," he said. "But elsewhere will your resurrection be." The elder said to him: "O holy youth, why do you keep God's many secrets to yourself? I perceive that the Holy Spirit is with you, and great power is hidden in you. You came to me to learn, and henceforth you will be my teacher. Therefore, from now on accept me as your monk and disciple. Say, then, where my resurrection will be." Brendan said to him: "Set out toward the east and where the wheels of your chariot break, build a place of prayer and abide. In that place many will rise together with you in glory." The bishop climbed into the chariot and, not far from his cell, as he made his way the chariot's two wheels were broken. And there was built Tuaym da Gualand [Tuam] monastery.[20]

Writing a monastic rule. (10) After this, St Brendan, like a busy bee, harvesting blossoms of holy virtue from various models, stored up in his heart, as if in a beehive dripping with sweetness, the honey of love and the wax of humility. Then, leaving Iarlaithe, he came to Mag nAí,[21] where an angel of the Lord, appearing to him, said: "Take up a sheet of parchment and write down the rule of living according to the will of God." There Brendan wrote, as the angel dictated, the indis-

18. Colmán mac Léinín, founder of Cloyne monastery (530–606), who, under Brendan's influence, reportedly abandoned a professional career as a secular poet to become a cleric. He is credited with composing early vernacular verse, ca. 565–604, some twenty lines of which survive. He is said to have bestowed his poetic skills on his foster son Dálach, from whom the Uí Dhálaigh (O'Daly) line of Connacht bardic poets descended. Ó Riain, *Dictionary*, 185–186. By renaming Colmanus *Columbe-manum*, Brendan may be taken to imply that Colmán had been misusing his skill, while as a religious his writing would reflect dovelike innocence. For Colmán see *AI* 68–69, 82–83; Ó Riain, *Dictionary*, 185–186.

19. *Brussels* 47 and *Lismore* 251 add that Brendan learned the monastic rules from him. They also give Iarlaithe's lineage.

20. Origin of the name is obscure. Tuaym may derive from Latin *tumulus* (burial mound), and the Irish "dá guála" suggests two shoulders, or hills, nearby. At the Synod of Kells-Mellifont in 1152, when the Irish church won papal recognition as a national institution, Tuam, with jurisdiction over Clonfert and Annaghdown, was one of four archdioceses to be established along with Armagh, Cashel, and Dublin. F.J. Byrne, "The Trembling Sod: Ireland in 1169," *NHI* 2: 1–42, at 42.

21. *R* 103 *campum Ae*; the Plain of Aí in Roscommon, Connacht.

pensable ecclesiastical rule to safeguard religious life, which is observed to this day in quite a few places.[22]

Evangelizing Connacht. (11) At that time, when the Lord wished to display Brendan's power to many, a dead youth was being carried to the grave while his parents and kin grieved him piteously. Moved by the lamentation, the man of profound kindness said: "Weep not, but rather trust in Christ, so that, as he first granted the spirit of life, he will see fit in the same way to raise the deceased." And drawing near the place, he prayed. At once, he who had been dead, arose. All who were there were amazed, and sorrow was turned to joy, and everyone there rejoiced, above all the youth's parents.

After this the man of God came to the king of the region and was honourably received by him.[23] He invited him to live wherever he might choose in his land. However, the true disdainer of the world declined this, having no desire to be advanced in this life's favours. So, returning a blessing for the offered gift, he went to the western region of Connacht as if to hide reports of his wondrous works. Passing through there for a time he converted very many to Christ through word and example, and he returned to Earc with many followers. His foster father rejoiced at the return of his protégé, and all his kinfolk and friends were filled with inexpressible joy. At length, already endowed with gifts of power by Christ the high priest, the disciple was raised to the priesthood by the bishop.[24]

Longing for a terra secreta. (12) But mindful of the command that was given Abraham, "Go forth out of thy country and from thy kindred" [Gen. 12:1–3], he burned with desire to go to a far country.[25] The Lord, seeing his misery from on high, gave him the following reply in a dream: "Brendan, your request is heard. Let it be done to you as your heart desires." Rejoicing in the revelation and leaving his men behind, he climbed a mountain at some remove from the sea.[26] And directing his gaze out on the surface of the sea, he saw a most delightful island, thoroughly suited to Christ's servants and very pleasing to him. There he fasted

22. Brendan's rule has not survived. Donnchadh Ó Corráin, *The Irish Church, Its Reform and the English Invasion* (Dublin, 2017), 10.

23. *S²* 327 adds: "at Cruachain" or Rathcrogan, in Roscommon, Connacht.

24. *M* 109 adds: "When he was made priest Brendan also became a monk. And many came to him from all over to forsake this world, and St Brendan made them monks. Later he founded monasteries and daughter houses in his own country, though not many at that time. When he returned from his voyage seeking the Promised Land of the Saints, then his *paruchia* (federation of monasteries) spread across Ireland." *M* 109 immediately adds, in rubricated letters: "Here begins the voyage of Brendan, the most holy father."

25. *S¹* 56 adds: "And he petitioned the Lord to give him a hidden land [*terra secreta*] in the sea, far removed from men."

26. Sliab n-Echtgne/Slieve Aughty on the Galway–Clare border. *S²* 327 has *montem Aitche*; *Lismore* 252 has Sliabh Daidche.

for three days to be certain of what he had seen. Again, as he slept, a voice from heaven resounded, saying: "Just as I promised the Israelite people a land, and I was present to help them attain it, so do I promise you the island that you saw. And I will accomplish this work."[27]

[The common version of the *Navigatio* begins here.]

Brendan's Voyage

Barinthus and the Isle of Delight. (13) He gave thanks to God for the promise of so great a gift. After pouring forth tears for the longest time, comforted by the Holy Spirit he returned to his company, saying: "My most beloved brothers and my fellow [spiritual] warriors, I seek your advice. For my heart is set on this: To carefully search for the promised land shown to me by heaven. Indeed, it is the land of the saints of which holy Barinthus spoke to us."[28]

Now, that I may reliably inform you of Barinthus' account of that land, it must be noted here what Barinthus, inspired by the Holy Spirit, related when he came one time to visit Brendan at the place known as the wood of Brendan's powers.[29] For as they were taking delight in conversing together, Barinthus prostrated himself on the ground and prayed for a long time as tears poured down his face. Lifting him from the ground, Brendan said: "Holy father, why are you sorrowful in the presence of your brothers? Did you not come to comfort us? Therefore, you ought to be cheerful in your countenance rather than sad. So, restore our spirits and tell us about the various wonders of God that you have seen and heard."

After Brendan's exhortations, Barinthus began to speak of an island in the ocean [the Isle of Delight], saying: "My brother Ternoc, fleeing the cares of

27. While Brendan's voyage in the *Vita* tradition appears originally to involve a search for a *terra secreta*, an isolated locale suited to monastic life, in the Rawlinson *Vita*, as in the *Navigatio*, he also clearly seeks the *terra repromissionis sanctorum*, the Promised Land of the Saints, an earthly paradise. Plummer, *LIS* 1: xvii–xviii; *VSH* 1: cxxii.

28. Possibly Bairrfhionn of Drumcullen in Offaly, who had a brother, Mearnóg or Tearnóg, better known as Earnán. Ó Riain, *Dictionary*, 83–84.

29. *R* 104 *Saltus uirtutum Brandani.* Commonly translated as Brendan's meadow of miracles, that is, Cluain Ferta or Clonfert. However, *R* may be employing *saltus* in the Vulgate sense of a forest or upland wood, 2 Kings 18:8, Is. 44:23, etc., not in the classical Latin sense of open meadow; *R*, like the Vulgate, Wis. 2:8, uses *pratum* for meadow (Chapter 76). The composer of *R* may have conceived of Barinthus as having visited Brendan in Kerry, perhaps at Ardfert, interpreted by some as "hill of miracles," after Brendan's return to Earc with many followers (11), and before his vision at Slieve Aughty (12).

working among the poor, sought out a place of hermitage.[30] Finding an island
in the sea well suited to heavenly contemplation, he decided to live there. After
a long time, many monks from all over began to join him. When he had gathered
there many brothers in Christ, and God had shown many wonders through him,
I hastened there to visit them. When I was three days away from their place,
inspired by the Spirit he hurried to meet me with his brothers and greeted us
with a holy kiss. When we had come to their hermitage, running from different
cells they greeted us with genuine affection. And although they had many
dwellings there, they shared one manner of life in faith, hope, and charity, and
one church, and one refectory.[31] Truly, no other food or drink was served there,
except the roots of plants and fruits of trees and drinking water to ease thirst.
After receiving refreshment from God, and when compline [the night prayer,
about 9 pm] was said, the brothers returned to their cells as was their custom
awaiting cock crow. As the rest gave themselves up to sleep or meditation, my
brother Ternoc and I, crossing the island, reached its western shore. On arriv-
ing, we found there a small, fitted-out boat. Then Ternoc said to me: 'Father, let
us board the boat and sail westward to the island called the Promised Land of
the Saints, which God will give to those who come after us in the end time.'[32]
After we had embarked and were sailing, fog overwhelmed us on every side so
that we scarcely could see the prow or stern of the small boat. After an hour or
so, a great light shone around us and a spacious land appeared, filled with vegetation, flowers, and fruits. Leaving the boat, we made the rounds of the island,
and though we tried for fifteen days we could not find the far side. And we saw
no plants there that were not in bloom, nor trees without fruit. Truly, the very
stones of the island were all of great worth.

30. *Brussels* 48 has Mernoc. His island, the *insula deliciosa*, has been identified as St
Earnán's Inis Caoin near Sliab Liacc/Slieve League on the Donegal coast. Ó Riain, *Dictionary*,
287. Later, at Chapter 66, Brendan revisits the *insulam, que vocabatur deliciosa vel deliciarum*.
See James Carney, "Review of *Navigatio Sancti Brendani Abbatis*, Edited with Introduction
and Notes by Carl Selmer," in *The Otherworld Voyage in Early Irish Literature*, ed. Jonathan M.
Wooding (Dublin, 2014), 42–51, at 44–45; and Ludwig Bieler, "Two Observations Concerning the *Navigatio Brendani*," in *Otherworld Voyage*, ed. Wooding, 90–93, at 92–93, with
reference to the mythical Inis Subai, the Isle of Joy.

31. *R* 105 *tamen erat conversatio in fide, spe et caritate*. The *Benedictine Rule*, Chapter 58,
refers to *conversatione morum suorum* (fidelity to monastic life). *The Rule of St. Benedict*, ed.
Timothy Fry (Collegeville, MN, 1981), 268–269.

32. *R* 105 *terra repromissionis sanctorum*. This concept harks back to God's covenant
with Abraham in Gen. 12:1–3. It is developed in Paul's letter to the Hebrews 11:8–16. Paul
writes that "By faith he that is called Abraham obeyed to go out into a place which he was to
receive for an inheritance ... . By faith he abode in the land of promise as in a strange country
... . For he looked for a city that hath foundations, whose builder and maker is God."

On the fifteenth day we came upon a river stretching from east to west. As we pondered all this, we could not decide what to do, nor how to proceed. After we deliberated among ourselves for a time, we decided to cross the river. But fearing to undertake anything without a sign from the Most High, we hoped for a divine answer. As we awaited divine counsel, a man of great brightness [an angel] suddenly appeared who greeted us, addressing us by our own names, saying: 'Well done, good brothers. The Lord has revealed this land to you, which He will give to his saints at the end of time. This river marks the middle of the island. Therefore, you may not go beyond. Accordingly, return to the place from which you came.' When he had said this, I asked him from what place he came, or what his name was. To which he said: 'Why do you ask from what place I come or what my name is? Why do you not ask me about this island that you see? For as you see it now, so has it remained from the beginning of the world.[33] It is always the same year on this island, and the same day, a day without the darkness of night. For our Lord Jesus Christ himself is the light.' After he finished saying all this, we immediately returned as we came, and the man with us, to the seashore where our boat was. As we boarded, the man vanished from our sight.

After this, crossing back through the fog, we came to the Isle of Delight, where the brothers awaited us.[34] When the brothers saw us, those who had previously grieved our absence exulted with great joy at our presence, saying: 'Why, fathers, did you leave your flock without a shepherd wandering on that island? Indeed, we knew that our abbot [Ternoc] often left us, though we knew not where he went. At times, he would remain away a month without us, at times two weeks, at times a week.' When I had heard this, I sought to comfort them, saying: 'Brothers, harbour nothing but good thoughts about this time. For indeed, your monastic life is before the gate of paradise. Close by lies the island called the Promised Land of the Saints where night never looms, nor day ends. That is the place to which Ternoc your abbot hastens at times. Angels of the Lord watch over that land. Can you not tell from the scent of our garments that we have been in God's paradise?' Then the brothers replied: 'Father, we knew you were in God's paradise, though we know not where it is.[35] For often we have noticed the fragrance of our abbot's clothes; indeed, his clothes often held a sweet smell for as much as forty days.' Then I said to the brothers: 'I was there with my brother Ternoc all that time without food or drink.' Yet we were so filled with spiritual

33. In the common version of the *Navigatio*, Barinthus and Ternoc are said to have spent a full year on the island, without food or drink. Giovanni Orlandi and Rossana E. Guglielmetti, eds., *Navigatio sancti Brendani: Alla scoperta dei segreti meravigliosi del mondo* (Florence, 2014), 6.
34. *R* 106 *insulam deliciosam.*
35. *R* 106 *Abba*, used for both father and abbot.

grace that to the brethren we seemed to be refreshed, even drunk, on new wine. I stayed forty days there [on the Isle of Delight] with the brothers. Then, having received the blessing of the abbot and community, I went back with my fellows to the cell to which I will return tomorrow, with the Lord's protection."

Having heard this, Brendan prostrated himself on the ground with all the company of brothers, glorifying God and saying: "The Lord, who revealed such marvels to his servants, is just in all his ways and holy in all his works [Ps. 144:17]. And blessed is God in his gifts who has nourished us this day with such spiritual food." After this, Brendan said: "Let us go now to refresh ourselves, and to the new commandment, that is, love" [Jn. 13:34]. When the night had run its course, in the morning Barinthus went back to his own cell with the brothers' blessing.

Brendan prepares to set out. (14) [After being granted a glimpse of the Promised Land of the Saints at 12], Brendan then said to his company: "What do you think? What would you advise? For in my heart, I have proposed to seek out the Promised Land of the Saints of which Barinthus spoke to us." Knowing the father's desire, they all said as if with one voice: "Father Abbot, your will is ours as well. Have we not forsaken our parents for you and God, and spurned our inheritances, and placed our wills and bodies in your hands? And so, we are ready to go with you, whether to life or to death, provided only that we seek to do the will of God." They all agreed that they would spend forty days in fasting and prayer, and thus protected by spiritual arms, seek the promised land. When the forty days were done, bidding farewell to [the rest of] the brothers and entrusting them to the prior of the monastery who later would succeed him there, the man of God travelled to the west coast with fourteen brothers to Inishmore [in the Aran Islands group in Galway], where holy Éanna lived at the time with his brothers, with whom Brendan the man of God stayed three days and three nights.[36]

Three late-coming monks. (15) After this, having received the blessing of Éanna and his monks, Brendan set out with his company for the region of Kerry where his parents were living. Yet not to visit them out of worldly affection but to make ready a vessel more conveniently there. He landed there at the foot of the mountain in the place which now is known as Brendan's Seat, where, setting up a tent, he stayed for a time.[37] Then Brendan and his company, equipped with iron tools, made ready a small boat with light pine wood ribs and frame, as is the custom in those parts, and covered it with ox hides dyed red, and caulked all the outer seams of the hides, and stowed provisions for forty days, and the other fittings required for the boat. When the boat was ready and the sail set, Brendan said to the brothers: "Board the boat in the name of the Father and of the Son and of the Holy

36. R 107 *insulam ... Aru.* Éanna founded a Christian settlement ca. 490 on the Aran Islands off Ireland's west coast.

37. R 107 *sedes Brandani.* Mount Brandon on the Dingle Peninsula in Kerry.

Spirit." As the brothers boldly boarded the boat and Brendan alone stood on the shore blessing the harbour, three monks came up from the monastery after them. At once, they fell to the ground at the feet of the man of God, saying: "Reverend father, allow us to accompany you, otherwise we will die here from hunger and thirst."[38] When the man of God saw their distress, he told them to board the boat. Because he knew what the future held for them, foretelling it he said: "I know, brothers, how you came here. This brother did well in coming, for God has prepared an exalted place for him. The second, though he will have gravely offended God, will obtain grace. But the third will be doomed for his obstinacy."[39]

Setting sail. (16) Whereupon Brendan boarded the boat, and with the sail spread, they steered [westward] toward the summer solstice. And having a favourable wind, they needed only to master the sail. After fifteen days, the wind died down and then the brothers rowed until their strength failed. Seeing them labour so, the man of God encouraged them, saying: "Brothers, do not exhaust yourselves. For the Lord is our helper and the pilot of our boat. Therefore, ship oars and rudder. Only leave the sail spread. Let the Lord do what he will with his servants and the boat. Fear then the Lord, for the Lord favours those who fear him" [Ps. 146:11]. After the disciples carried out the father's orders, in the evening they refreshed themselves. For this was their custom, always to eat in the evening. And whenever they caught a wind, they would stop rowing. But they never knew from which direction it came, or where it would lead them.

First landing, on the island of the Faithful Steward. (17) After forty days like this, when they had exhausted their provisions and were trusting in God alone for help, an island appeared to the north, very rocky and high. As they drew near the shore, they spied an extremely high bank, like a wall, and various streams flowing down from the island's summit into the sea. As the brothers could not find a place where they might readily land, on account of the cliff's steepness, then, afflicted by hunger and thirst, they took up their flasks to draw some of the flowing water to ease their thirst. When Brendan had seen this, he forbade them the water, saying: "Brothers, what you are doing is folly. Since our God does not want to show us a place to land on the island, therefore do not carry off water from it, or anything else. Be patient. For our Lord Jesus Christ, who does not fail those who trust in him, will show his servants a landing place three days from now and a fitting place to stay for a time so that our bodies can be refreshed." When they had sailed around the island for three days, on the third day at about the ninth hour

38. In ancient Irish fashion, the monks threaten to fast against Brendan – that is, go on a hunger strike – to obtain his consent.

39. A sin generally taken to involve a rejection of the Holy Spirit. In this case, the monk insists on joining the voyage despite Brendan's prophetic warning that the voyage will not go well for him.

[3 pm] they found a landing place where there was access for one boat. When the holy man saw the desired haven, he stood and blessed the entry. It was a rock cut of great height on both sides, like a wall. As the brothers went up to land from the boat, the holy pastor warned them not to carry away gear with them from the boat.

The marvellous palace. (18) As they were walking by the sea cliffs, a dog met them, that, coming to Brendan's feet, fawned on him as dogs do when their masters arrive [Tob. 11:9]. Seeing the dog stretched out in a friendly manner, the man of God like a second Tobias said to his company: "Has our God not given us a good messenger? Then let us follow him" [Tob. 5:5]. So, they accompanied the dog, which went before them to a town on the island. Entering the town, they saw a lofty and spacious court furnished with made-up couches and chairs, and with water for foot washing. When they had sat down, the man of God cautioned the brothers not to wrongfully take away any of the furnishings of the house. He said: "Beware brothers, lest Satan lead you into temptation. For I see that he is urging one of the three who came after us from the monastery to grave theft. Pray, then, for his soul, as his flesh has been given over to Satan's power." For the walls of the house in which they were staying were hung about with suspended vessels of various kinds of metal, with bridles, and with horns enclosed in silver.

Satan tempts a brother. (19) Then Brendan said to the attendant who customarily set food before him: "Bring the meal that God, ever compassionate, ever good, has sent us." As the brother got up to serve, he found the table set and covered with a tablecloth and enough dazzlingly white loaves and fishes to ease their hunger. When everything was ready the holy father blessed the heaven-sent meal, saying: "Give glory to the God of heaven, who gives food to all flesh" [Ps. 135:25–26]. The brothers sat and ate their food with fear and love of God. And they took as much drink as they needed. When the meal was done, along with thanksgiving and the divine praises, the holy pastor said to the brothers: "Now rest. See, here are individual beds well made up for each of you. You need to rest your limbs after great toil." However, as the brothers slept, Brendan saw Satan in the guise of a black Ethiopian, holding a bridle in his hand, and calling to the brother to take it, which he did.[40] He seized the bridle and gave in to the occasion of temptation. When the man of God saw that, he rose from the bed and remained in prayer until the next day. In the morning, after the divine office of lauds [the dawn prayers] were concluded, they hastened to the boat. And behold, a meal appeared as on the first day, fully prepared. And so, God supplied food for his servants for three days and as many nights.

40. R 109 *frenum*. A bridle chased with silver. Carl Selmer suggested it may designate a necklace. Carl Selmer, ed., *Navigatio Sancti Brendani Abbatis: From Early Latin Manuscripts* (Notre Dame, 1959; repr. Dublin, 1989), 85 n27.

First late-coming monk dies, absolved. (20) After this, Brendan set out with his company for the boat. He said to the company: "See that none of you takes away with him anything that belongs to this island." And they all said: "God forbid, Father, that any furtive theft should taint our journey." Then Brendan added: "See, our brother of whom I spoke to you yesterday has a bridle ornamented with silver in his bosom, which he foolishly stole last night at the devil's urging." When the brother heard that, he cast the bridle from his breast and prostrated himself at the feet of the man of God saying: "Father, I have sinned. Forgive me and pray that my soul be not lost." Seeing this, the brothers immediately prostrated themselves on the ground, pleading for his soul. When the holy pastor lifted them up from the ground, they saw a little Ethiopian leap from that brother's bosom, who said in a loud and mournful voice: "Man of God, why do you expel me from my lodging where I have dwelt seven years, and dispossess me now of my inheritance?" Hearing that voice, Brendan the herald of truth said: "I command you on the part of Christ, whom I serve, that you harm no human being until the day of judgment." After that, turning to the brother, he said: "Take the Lord's body and blood, for your soul will now leave your body, and you will be buried here. Because of your contrition and our insistent prayers, your sin is forgiven. However, your brother who came with you from our monastery will have a burial place in hell." Accordingly, having received the Eucharist as prudent Viaticum [part of the last rites for the dying] for the journey, the brother's soul left the body and was received by angels of light in the brothers' sight. And his body was buried in that place by the brothers.

The Steward greets them. (21) After this, they went to the place where they had left their boat. As they were boarding, a young man [the Faithful Steward] came to them carrying a basket full of loaves of bread and a pitcher of fresh water. He said to them: "Accept a gift from your servant's hand. For a long journey still awaits you until you find comfort. From now until Easter this supply of bread and water will not fail." Then, having received the good messenger's blessing, they sailed the ocean, where God chose to lead them. And they took food every second day.

The Isle of Sheep. (22) As they were led through distant reaches of the ocean in this way, one day they saw an island [the Isle of Sheep] not far from them. As they rowed hard to reach it, God sent them a longed-for wind so that they did not have to toil so. When they had successfully landed at the harbour, the man of God told the brothers to disembark, and he followed them. As they went about the island, they saw abundant streams full of fishes flowing from various springs. Brendan then said to the brothers: "Let us say Mass here, offering to God the spotless Lamb, for today is the day of the Lord's Supper [Holy Thursday]." When they had done this, they stayed there until Holy Saturday. Making the rounds of the island, they saw various flocks of white sheep, so numerous that they could scarcely see the ground for the size of the flocks. Then Brendan said to the brothers: "Take from these flocks what is needed for the feast day. For the earth is the Lord's, and the fullness thereof" [Ps. 23:1]. Carrying out the command, they took a sheep from the flock and, bound by the horns, it followed them as if it were tame until they came to the place where the man of God was. Again, the holy pastor commanded one of the brothers to go to the flock and bring away a spotless lamb from it. The brother hastened to carry out the order, leading back with him the spotless lamb.

The Steward supplies them. (23) When they had readied everything for the next day's service [on Good Friday], the aforesaid man appeared, carrying a hamper full of loaves baked under the ashes, and the other things that were required. After he had placed this before the man of God, he fell on his face three times saying: "How have I deserved, O pearl of God, that you should be fed from the labour of my hands during these holy days?" Brendan lifted him from the ground, kissed him, and said: "Son, tell us where our Lord Jesus Christ wants us to observe his holy resurrection." The man replied: "Father, you will observe Holy Saturday here. Tomorrow [Saturday evening] you must observe your [Easter] vigils and Masses on that island which you see. For that is the Lord's desire, who disposes all things well" [Wis. 8:1]. When he had said this, he began humbly to serve God's servants and to prepare all that was required for the following day. When everything was ready and brought to the boat [on Holy Saturday], the Faithful Steward said to Brendan: "Your boat now cannot carry any more. But after eight days I will send you all that will be required until Pentecost." Then Brendan said: "How will you know where we may be staying after eight days?" And he said: "Tonight you will be on that island that you see nearby, and there tomorrow until the sixth hour [noon]. Then you will sail to the island not far to the west of it, called the Paradise of Birds, where you will stay until the octave of Pentecost." Brendan also asked him about the sheep they saw on the island, how they could be so large. For they were as large as oxen. He replied: "No one milks the sheep on this island, nor does winter's storm harry them, and they abide day and night ever grazing. Therefore, they are larger than in your country." Then, having shared a meal and a blessing, they went to the boat and made for the island foreshown to them.

Easter on Casconius. (24) When they approached it, the boat came to rest before they could reach a landing place. Then Brendan ordered the brothers to go into the sea, to lead the boat with ropes to the longed-for haven. And so, it was done. The island was very rough, without any vegetation, and on its shore no sand was to be found. As the brothers spent the night [of the Easter vigil] in prayer and vigils on the island, Brendan alone remained in the boat. For he knew what manner of isle it was. In truth, it was not an island. But God Almighty, to whose will every creature bends, caused a great whale to raise its back above the sea, to be a suitable place for his servants to spend the night of his resurrection. Therefore, the man of God was loath to tell the brothers what sort of place it was where they had spent that night lest, terrified, they wavered in faith. In the morning [on Easter Sunday], the holy pastor told all the priests to sing their Masses individually, which they did. While the reverend father celebrated Mass in the boat, the brothers carried from it meats and fishes that they had brought from the other island, to preserve with salt, and also to cook some of it. When they had done this, they set a cauldron on the fire and when the cauldron began to boil, the island began to stir. Feeling the island's motion, the brothers rushed for the boat, pleading for their protector's help. The man of God hauled them aboard by hand, one by one, and so they set sail, leaving behind on the island everything they had prepared.

The island then was borne out on the ocean, and they could see the burning fire 2,000 paces [two miles] away on the sea. Then the holy man disclosed his secret to them and explained what manner of island it was, saying: "Brothers, do you wonder at what this island has done, moving in this way across the sea?" The brothers said: "We are astonished, and also terrified, at its motion." He said to them: "My sons, don't be frightened. For last night God revealed to me in a vision the secret of this matter. For it was not an island on which you were staying, but the greatest of all sea creatures, which forever seeks to join its head and tail but cannot because of its length. And Casconius is its name."[41]

The Paradise of Birds. (25) After this they found a very delightful island [the Paradise of Birds] full of grasses, flowers, and trees abounding in fruit. As they sought a port to put into, at the southern end of the island they found a freshwater stream flowing into the sea, and there they brought the boat to land. As they disembarked, Brendan instructed the brothers to haul the boat upstream with ropes as far as they might. The stream was about one boat-length wide. The brothers did as their father directed, hauling the boat up to the fresh spring from which the stream flowed. Then Brendan said to the brothers: "Our Lord Jesus Christ, truly good, truly kind, has given us a place to stay for his holy resurrection [the Easter octave]. My brothers, if we had nothing else to refresh us, this spring alone would suffice us as food and drink."

The birds' fall from grace. (26) Over the spring there was a remarkably tall tree, covered with radiant white birds. They so covered the tree that human eyes could

---

41. Echoes Irish "cáisc," for Easter. Possibly with an echo of Latin *cascus* (the ancient one). *Anglie* 142 has *Iasconius*, derived from Irish "iasc" (fish). Early Christians used the Greek word for fish, *IXΘΥΣ*, as an acrostic for Ἰησοῦς Χριστός Θεοῦ Υἱός Σωτήρ, "Jesus Christ, Son of God, Saviour."

The Life of St Brendan | 49

scarcely make it out in full. When the man of God caught sight of this, he pondered inwardly what caused such a multitude of birds to be gathered in one tree. His pondering so vexed him that he wept for help resolving his uncertainty, saying: "God, you who discern reins [minds] and hearts [Ps. 7:9–10] and who lay bare hidden things, you know my heart's anguish. Therefore, I implore your majesty, that through your great mercy you deign to reveal to me your secret concerning these birds which lies hidden from me. Father, I do not rely on my own worth or merit in this matter, but I trust in your indulgence to clear up the uncertainty of this message." As the man of heavenly desires spoke to himself, one of the birds flew from the tree, its wings echoing off the boat like little bells. Perching forward on the boat's prow, it stretched out its wings in a show of interior joy and looked on the man of God with a peaceful expression. The man of God knew at once that the Lord was mindful of his pleas, and he said to the bird: "Because you are a servant of God and a herald, therefore tell us from where you came here, and how such a vast crowd of birds should be gathered together here." The bird said to him: "We are from the great fall of the ancient foe, who were not fully of the same mind as him.[42] But because we consented in part to his sin, catastrophe befell us too. Truly, God is just, and true, and merciful. For that reason, in his judgment he sent us to this place where we suffer no other punishments, save that we cannot see the presence of God.[43] For to that extent he banished us from the fellowship of others who stood more firmly. On feast days and on Sundays we take on bodies such as you see, and we abide here praising our Creator. Like other spirits who are sent through different regions of the earth and sky, so also can we move about. You and your brothers have been one year on your journey. Six more years await. Where you observed Easter today, there likewise will you observe it every year of your travels. Afterwards, you will find what you have set your heart on, the Promised Land of the Saints." When the bird had spoken these words, it alighted from the prow and flew back to the others.

Singing the hours. (27) When the hour of vespers [6 pm] had come, all the birds in the tree sang out as with one voice, beating their wings on their sides and saying: "A hymn, O God, becometh thee in Zion, and a vow shall be paid to thee in Jerusalem" [Ps. 64:2]. They repeated the short verse for about the span of an hour. To the brothers, the melody and the sound of their wings seemed like some

---

42. The reference is to the fall of Lucifer during the war in heaven. Apoc. 12:7–9.

43. The notion that some of the fallen angels are spared the torments of hell, while popular in the medieval era, was unorthodox. Thomas Aquinas, writing around 1265 of the fallen angels who, "once they have sinned, are fixed in sin" because the angelic will is unchanging, expounded the orthodox view that "God's mercy delivers the repentant from their sins, but not those who cannot repent because of a changeless attachment to evil." Thomas Aquinas, *Summa Theologiae* 1.64.2, Blackfriars ed. (New York, London, 1964–1981), 9: 290–291.

sweet lament. Then Brendan said to the brothers: "Refresh your bodies. For today your souls were filled with divine nourishment." When the meal was over, the brothers observed the divine office [compline, about 9 pm], then they rested until the third watch of the night [midnight]. Waking, the man of God roused the brothers for the vigils of the holy night [matins at midnight, and lauds]. As he began to recite the short verse: "O Lord, thou wilt open my lips, and my mouth shall declare thy praise" [Ps. 50:17], the birds sounded together with voice and wing, saying: "Praise ye the Lord all his angels, praise ye him all his hosts" [Ps. 148:2]. They sang for an hour, as they had at vespers. When dawn put an end to night, they all sang: "And let the brightness of the Lord God be upon us" [Ps. 89:17], singing the psalms [at prime, 6 am] in the same melody and for the same length of time as at morning lauds. At the hour of terce [9 am] they sang this short verse: "Sing praises to our God, sing praises to our king, sing ye wisely" [Ps. 46:7–8]. At sext [noon] they sang: "Lord, let your face shine upon us, and have mercy on us" [Ps. 66:2]. At the ninth hour [3 pm] they said: "Behold how good and how pleasant it is for brethren to dwell together in unity" [Ps. 132:1]. In this way, the birds rendered praise to God, day and night. They stayed there, praising God through the octave of the feast.

Their seasonal travels. (28) When the Easter festival was over, Brendan said to his company: "Draw water from this spring." When the brothers had done so, the man arrived with whom they had been the three days before Easter, carrying with him in his boat enough food and drink for them. When everything was brought from the boat in the presence of the man of God, he [the Steward] spoke to them, saying: "My brothers, here you have enough until the holy day of Pentecost. Do not drink [directly] from this spring, for it is potent indeed to drink [while flowing]. I shall tell you about its nature. Sleep will immediately fall upon whomever drinks [directly] from it, and he will not awaken for twenty-four hours. Yet when it is drawn out of the spring, it has the nature and taste of water."[44] Having said this, receiving the holy father's blessing he returned to his place.

They stayed there until the feast of Pentecost. And the sweet singing of the birds delighted and revived them. On Holy Pentecost, the Steward came to them bringing with him such things as were necessary for the feast day. When they sat down together for the meal, the Steward spoke, saying: "Because you still have a long journey ahead, take this water in your vessels, and such bread as you can

44. Compare with the incident in Chapter 36. While the water is dangerously potent while flowing, the implication is that it loses its potency when it has been drawn out in a container and is still. In Judg. 7:5–7, the Lord instructs Gideon to select his warriors from among those who drink at the spring of Harod by "casting it [cupped] with the hand to their mouth" and removing it from the spring, rather than those who kneel to drink directly from the flowing waters.

keep. Next year, God willing, I will call upon you." When he had said that, receiving a blessing from the holy man [Brendan] he returned to his place. When the octave of the feast was over the holy man instructed his company to ready the boat and to fill their vessels from the spring. When everything the Steward [had previously] directed was ready, then the aforesaid bird [from Chapter 26] came flying swiftly back and perched again on the prow of the boat. As if to strengthen them against the sea's perils, it said: "You should know that, where you were on Holy Thursday this past year, there likewise will you be this year on that same night. And just as you were on Casconius' back on Holy Saturday night, so will you be this year on that night. In eight months, you will reach the island known as the Isle of the Community of Ailbhe [of Emly in Tipperary] where you will observe the Lord's Nativity."[45] When the bird had foretold this, it returned to its place.

Ailbhe's island. (29) The brothers then spread the sheet and set sail. The birds, too, sang together, saying: "Hear us, O God, our saviour, who art the hope of all the ends of the earth, and in the sea afar off" [Ps. 64:6]. Then they were borne across the breadth of the great sea for three months and could see nothing but sky and sea. One day an island appeared, not far off. As they drew near the shore, a rush of wind dragged them away from the harbour, and so they sailed for forty days around the island, nor could they find a landing. As the brothers were nearly exhausted, they pleaded tearfully with the Lord in his goodness and compassion to come to their aid. After they had spent three days in prayer and fasting, a narrow passage appeared where there was space for a single boat. Two springs appeared there as well, one of which was muddy and the other clear. Then the brothers hastened with flasks to draw water. Seeing this, Brendan said to them: "My sons, do not do anything here without the consent of the elders who abide on this island. For the water you wish to steal without the consent of the elders, you can obtain by their leave." So, on the father's order the brothers left the water they craved.

Ailbhe's monastery. (30) When they had left the boat a very dignified old man met them whose face shone, and whose hair was the colour of snow. He prostrated himself three times on the ground before he kissed the man of God. Brendan lifted him from the ground. As they kissed one another, the old man took Brendan's hand, and proceeding that way they went to the monastery. When they were before the monastery gate, Brendan halted with his company and said to the elder: "Whose monastery is this? Who is in charge? And from where do those who live here come?" And while he put various questions in this way to the old man, yet he got no reply from him, except that he made

45. R 115 *insula familie Helvei.*

known with his hand that they should be silent. When the man of God discerned from the signals that this was a silent retreat, he cautioned the brothers, saying: "Keep your mouths from breaking the silence, lest these people be vexed in any way by your chatter." That said, eleven brothers from the monastery met them with crosses and hymns, saying: "Rise up, holy ones, from your dwelling places and advance in the way of truth. Sanctify the place, bless the people, that the Lord may think fit to keep us your servants in peace."[46] When the short verse was said, they gave one another the kiss of peace. Then the brothers of the monastery led them to the oratory, that there they might first seek the kingdom of God [Mt. 6:33]. After this, the abbot of the monastery with his monks washed the guests' feet, singing: "A new commandment I give unto you," and the rest [Jn. 13:34].

The monastery's abundance. (31) That done, the guests were led to the refectory where they were refreshed with wonderfully white bread and some incredibly tasty roots, in deepest affection, great gravity, and silence. A whole loaf of bread and a pot of spring water was placed between each pair of them by the server who tended table. Then the abbot of the monastery with great gravity said: "You may now drink with an easy mind from this spring, from which you wished earlier to draw water without permission. From the other spring that you saw, the muddy one, the brothers' feet are washed as need be, for it is always warm. We know not where the loaves that you see at our table are prepared, nor who carries them to our storeroom. Yet it is clear to us that they are served to us out of God's abundant goodness by some obedient creature of his. We, too, who are here, twenty-four brethren of the religious house, have twelve loaves daily such as you see, so that one always feeds two. On great feast days and Sundays, the supply of bread is doubled so that everyone may have a meal from the leftovers. Now, too, on your arrival the supply of bread was doubled. God has nourished us in this manner for eighty years, from the time of Patrick and holy Ailbhe our father until now.[47] No signs of old age or feebleness ever trouble us, but, as you see, we serve God, day and night, without any hindrance. Moreover, on this island we need no fire to prepare our food or to warm us. No cold or heat afflicts us here. When the time comes for the morning vigils, our lamps that we brought with us from our own country are kindled by divine breath, and none of them is diminished until day."

---

46. Echoing the ancient processional chant: *Surgite sancti de mansionibus vestris loca sanctificate plebem benedicite et nos humiles peccatores in pace custodite.*

47. Ailbhe, too, was reputed to have been a pilgrim to the Land of Promise. Ó Riain, *Dictionary,* 59. See also *AI* 68–69; *AU* 66–67, 70–71, 72–73; and Pádraig Ó Riain, ed., *Beatha Ailbhe: The Life of Saint Ailbhe of Cashel and Emly* (London, 2017), 35.

The monks' strict silence. (32) After this pleasant meal, they drank three times, and the abbot sounded a signal.[48] The brothers, rising from the table with silence and gravity, hastened to the church with divine praise. The two holy men walked behind the others. As they entered the church, twelve other brothers came out of the church from the opposite direction and genuflected before the holy fathers. Then Brendan said to the abbot of the monastery: "Father abbot, why were these not fed at the same time as us?" The abbot replied: "They were not fed with us because our table cannot seat us together at the same time. Now they will be refreshed and will want nothing. And we who are going into the church will sing vespers, so that our brothers can likewise sing after us."

When vespers were concluded, Brendan pondered how the church was constructed. It was square, the same in length and width, and it had seven lamps: three before the central altar and two before each of the other two altars. The altars were made of crystal, and so were their vessels, the patens and chalices and cruets and other vessels pertaining to divine worship, and there were twenty-four seats round about. The abbot sat between the two choirs, and he always led the holy office. In the monastery, no voice or noise was heard. Nor did anyone presume to do anything without an elder's approval. If any of the brothers needed to carry out some essential task, he humbly genuflected before the abbot, making his intentions known through appropriate signs. Then the abbot, taking up a stylus and tablet and writing out his wishes, signalled the petitioner to read it. When Brendan had carefully considered all this, the abbot said to him: "My father, now it is time that we return to the refectory so that everything may be done while there is light." And so they did, returning to the refectory. When everything was carried out there that was required for bodily refreshment, they all hastened with great gravity to compline. When the abbot had begun the short verse "Attend unto my help, O Lord" [Ps. 37:23], and they all also had paid homage to the ever-blessed Trinity and had sung the whole office of compline with devotion, the brothers all went forth to their cells respectfully leading their guests with them, in whom they deemed to be lodging Christ himself [Mt. 25:37–40].[49]

Brendan may not stay. (33) The abbot and Brendan stayed in the church awaiting the coming of the light. Brendan questioned the abbot about the brothers' silence and community life, how they kept such strict silence, and how they kept such a hard life living in human flesh. The abbot replied with great humility

---

48. Three times, to honour the Trinity.

49. Mt. 10:40–42. The *Life of Crónán of Roscrea* has monks welcoming "Christ in a guest" and treating guests as they would Christ. Pádraig Ó Riain, trans., *Four Tipperary Saints* (Dublin, 2014), 35–36. The *Benedictine Rule*, 53:1, states: "All guests who present themselves are to be welcomed as Christ." Fry, *Rule*, 255.

and deference: "My father, I confess before my Christ that it has been eighty years since we came to this island, and we have heard no human voice except when we sing the praises of our God. Among us no voice is raised. But only through a sign made with a finger or the eyes is what is needful expressed, and this is done only by the elders. None of us has suffered any physical or spiritual infirmity since we came to this place." Hearing of so excellent a manner of living in community, Brendan burst out in these heartfelt words, saying: "My father, may we live here together with you?" The abbot replied: "It is not permitted. For it is not the will of God." And he added: "And Father Brendan, why do you ask me about this matter? Did not God reveal to you before you came here what you must do? Indeed, you must return to your own country with your fourteen brothers, for God has prepared there in your monastery the place for your burial. Of the two remaining [brothers], one will sojourn abroad on the isle of the anchorites. The other will be condemned by a most foul death to hell."

Spiritual light. (34) As they were conversing thus together, as they looked on, something like a flaming arrow was loosed through a window that set alight all the church lamps. When the lamps were lit the arrow immediately went out by the same way. Again, Brendan inquired by whom those lights were quenched in the morning. And the abbot said to him: "Come and see the mystery of this thing of which you inquire. Behold, you see the candles burning in the middle of the vessels. Yet none of them will be consumed or be diminished, nor will any ash remain in the morning. For the light is spiritual." Brendan then said: "How can a spiritual or incorporeal light burn in the material world?" The elder replied: "Have you not considered the burning bush on Mount Sinai, and yet the bush remained unharmed by fire?" [Ex. 3:2].[50]

They leave Ailbhe's island. (35) After the holy men kept watch all through the night until morning, Brendan sought leave to depart. The elder said to him: "My father Brendan, you must observe Christmas with us and stay until the octave of Epiphany." Brendan bowed to the petitioner's entreaties and stayed the time specified by the father. When the designated feast days were over, Brendan and his company boarded their boat and entrusted themselves and their journey to God the pilot, having received provisions from the monastery and the blessing of those holy men. And they were borne hither and yon in this manner through ocean byways until the beginning of Lent.[51]

---

50. S^1 62 adds: "Brendan said: 'But I have read it.' And he said to him: 'If so, trust in God always, for the reward is given to those who watch through the night.'" [Lk. 12:38]

51. Marking the start of their second year at sea.

The Second Year at Sea

The stupor-inducing spring. (36) Then one day they saw an island not far from them. When the brothers had seen it, they rowed hard. For by now they were nearly exhausted from hunger and thirst because their food and water had given out three days earlier. When they reached the island, Brendan blessed the landing place, so they might safely put ashore. While crossing the island, they came upon an extraordinarily clear spring from which various kinds of fishes were swimming down to the sea. The holy pastor said to the brothers: "Sons, take notice and understand how God our comforter gave us this place of rest and comfort after much toil. Take enough fish for our meal and gather herbs and spring roots that the Lord has provided for his servants." When the disciples had carried out everything according to the master's order, he said again to them: "Take care, brothers, that you do not make excessive use of these waters lest your bodies be heavily troubled." As the brothers did not heed the force of the father's precept about drinking the water, but some of them drank single cups, others two, and some three, immediately a three-day stupor fell over those who drank three cups, and two days on those who drank two, and a day and a night on those who drank one. Brendan pleaded with God without pause on behalf of the brothers because through ignorance they chanced to fall into such peril.

The curdled sea. (37) After these three days, the father said to his sons: "Beloved ones, let us flee this mortal peril lest something worse befall us. For God provided sustenance for our needs, and you then turned it to your misfortune. Therefore, let us leave this island, taking enough fish to last three days until Holy Thursday, and likewise enough roots for these three days, and no more." Loading the boat with everything as Brendan had instructed, they sailed the ocean in a northerly direction. After three days and nights, the wind having failed, the sea became thick as curds because of the great calm. Brendan instructed his company to stop rowing and let God direct the boat. When the brothers did so, the boat was borne through diverse reaches of the ocean for about twenty days. And always, they ate every third day.[52]

Second Holy Thursday at sea. (38) One day an island appeared so far off that it seemed to them like some clouds. And Brendan said to his company: "My sons, do you recognize that island?" They replied: "We don't, father." Then he said: "I recognize it. For it is the island [the Isle of Sheep] where we were last year on

---

52. Time appears to stand still for them during this second Lenten season at sea. Brendan announces it is three days until Holy Thursday. However, they sail for three days, encounter the curdled sea, where they drift for twenty days, then reach the island of the Steward on Holy Thursday. Moreover, their three-day supply of food lasts the entire time, and they eat every third day.

Holy Thursday, where the good Steward abides." Hearing that, the brothers rowed furiously, so that they might quickly reach the restful place. When the holy father saw this, he said: "Brothers, do not weary your limbs so with excessive labour, but let God the pilot guide the boat. Give over the boat to him to manage who forsakes no one unless he is first forsaken, who fails no one unless he is failed by his servant." When the brothers heeded the advice, as they drew near the shore the Steward came to meet them in a small boat and led them to the landing place where they had disembarked the year before, glorifying God and kissing their feet one by one, beginning with Brendan down to the last one, saying: "God is wonderful in his saints; the God of Israel is he who will give power and strength to his people. Blessed be God" [Ps. 67:36]. When the short verse was concluded, and the brothers' gear was brought from the boat, he set up a tent and prepared a bath, for it was Holy Thursday. Then he clothed all the brothers in fresh garments and so served them for three days. The brothers observed the Lord's Passion [the Good Friday service] in that place with great care, waiting there until Holy Saturday.

Second Easter on Casconius. (39) When the Holy Saturday offices were concluded, the saving hosts rendered to God [Easter vigil Masses celebrated], and the meal taken, the Steward said to them: "Go and board your boat so that you may observe Easter Sunday where you observed it last year [on Casconius], staying there until the sixth hour. After that, you will reach the island called the Paradise of Birds, where you were last year at this time until the octave of Pentecost. Take with you, too, all the food and drink that is required in the meantime. For with God's assistance, I will visit you a week Sunday." He loaded the boat with food and drink, as much as it would hold. Then, having blessed each other, they boarded the boat and set sail for the other island. As they drew near the place where they were meant to land, the cooking pot appeared that they had left there the year before. Then Brendan, disembarking from the boat with his company, sang the hymn of the three youths to the end.[53] When the hymn was concluded the man of God cautioned the brothers, saying: "O my sons, watch and pray that you do not enter into temptation [Mt. 26:41]. For consider how God has subjected the vast beast under us without any hindrance." As the sons were strengthened in faith by the father's words so that they no longer so greatly feared the beast's motion, they remained, here and there on the island, praising God without pause through the night until early [Easter] morning. When the brothers assembled in the morning, the priests each offered the saving host to God until the third hour [9 am]. Then Brendan the man of God offered the spotless Lamb

---

53. The Canticle of the Three Servants in the Fiery Furnace, Dan. 3:51–90, associated from ancient times with the Easter vigil and the resurrection.

to God [celebrated Mass], saying: "Last year I observed Easter here. I intend to do the same this year." When everything had been completed there that pertained to the Lord's Resurrection, they went to the isle of the birds as they had the year before.

Second Easter octave. (40) As they drew near the landing place, all the birds of the island, crying out harmoniously in human voices, said: "Salvation to our God, who sitteth upon the throne, and to the Lamb" [Apoc. 7:10]. And again: "The Lord is God, and he hath shone upon us. Appoint a solemn day with shady boughs, even to the horn of the altar" [Ps. 117:27]. They repeated these words every half hour until the holy man and his company retired to his tent. When they had completed the Easter feasts there until the Easter octave, the Steward came on Low Sunday [the Sunday after Easter], as he had promised, bringing with him what was required for the use of Christ's poor.

God's plan for the voyage. (41) As they sat at table, the aforesaid bird [from 26, 28] perched on the prow of the boat, making a noise with its outstretched wings like the sound of a great organ. The man of God then discerned that it wished to tell him something. As the brothers listened attentively to the bird's voice, it said to them: "God has ordained four moments in time for you until the seven years of your travel are come to an end. Every year on Holy Thursday, you shall be with your Steward, who is here. You will observe Easter on the monster's back. But you shall remain with us on this island until the octave of Pentecost. You will observe Christmas with Ailbhe's community.[54] When the seven years of your journey have ended, with its many prior trials, you will find the Promised Land of the Saints that you earnestly seek. There will you stay forty days. Then God will lead you back to the land of your birth." When he heard this, Brendan prostrated himself on the ground giving thanks to his Saviour. Having done these things, the bird returned to its place.

They sail again. (42) When the brothers had finished eating, the Steward said to them: "God willing and helping, I will return to you on the day of the coming of the Holy Spirit upon the apostles [Pentecost], with fit provisions for your needs." After receiving a blessing from Brendan and the rest of the brothers, the Steward went back to his own place. They stayed there for the time he ordained for them. When the feast days were over, the man of God told his company to get ready to resume the journey and to fill their containers from the spring. When everything that was needed for the voyage was ready, the Steward came to them with his boat full of food and drink. Stowing what he had brought in the boat, he

54. *Brussels* 59 also says Brendan's year will fall into four moments in time: Holy Thursday with the Steward; Easter on the back of the sea beast; from Easter to Pentecost with the fallen angels; and with the monks of Ailbhe's community from Christmas to Candlemas on Feb. 2, marking Jesus' presentation in the temple and Mary's purification.

kissed each of the brothers, and returned to his own island. Then sailing for forty days through uncharted seas, they struggled to make their way.

A sea beast attacks them. (43) One day as they were sailing in this way, a huge sea monster appeared behind them that rushed at great speed to devour them, spouting billows of water from its nostrils and stirring the sea like a raging storm. As the brothers were thrown into confusion when they saw this dreadful turbulence at sea, Brendan, ever trusting in his Lord, said: "Fear not, you who are of little faith. Did not Peter the apostle walk on the waters so long as he did not doubt? But as soon as he faltered in faith, he began to sink [Mt. 14:28–31]. God, who is ever our protector, will himself deliver us from the maw of this beast. And not only will he preserve us from the assault of this monster, but from all the perils of this sea."

A second beast defends them. (44) As the beast drew near them, huge waves from it surged at the boat so that the brothers were even more terrified. The venerable elder, raising his hands to heaven, said: "Lord, deliver us as you delivered David from the hand of the giant Goliath [1 Kings 17:38–50]. Lord, deliver us as you freed Daniel from the lions' maws in the pit [Dan. 6:16–24]. Lord, deliver us as you delivered Jonah the prophet from the belly of the great whale, when he was there for three days and as many nights" [Jon. 2:1–11]. When the prayer was ended, another monster, coming from the west and spouting flame from its mouth, fiercely attacked the other. Brendan then said to the brothers: "See, children, the wonderful works of God Almighty, and consider the obedience the creature pays to the Creator. Now, beloved ones, await the outcome of this struggle, for one beast fights the other beast on our behalf, and no harm will come to us. Rather this occasion will serve to glorify our God." That said, the beast pursuing them was cut into three pieces in front of them, and the other went back after its victory to the place from which it had come.

They feast on the beast. (45) The next day they saw a very pleasant island, full of trees. Drawing near it, they saw part of the slain beast on the seashore. Brendan said to the brothers: "Behold part of that beast that wanted to devour us. Now, consume it and be restored with its flesh. For you will be delayed a long time on this island. Therefore, haul our boat to higher ground and seek a suitable place for your tent." When the brothers had carried out all this, the holy father said to them: "Now, beloved ones, take enough of this monster's flesh to suffice you for three months. For tonight the corpse of this monster will be devoured by other beasts." When all this was done, the disciples said to Brendan: "Father abbot, how can we live here without water?" He said to them: "Is it harder for God to give us water than nourishment? For he who provided food will also provide drink." Again, he said to them: "Go now to the south shore of the island and there you will find a spring of fresh water and many herbs. Take from them all, in moderation." Going out, the brothers found everything as the man of God foretold.

Marooned. (46) Then they stayed on that island for three months, for there was a great storm all that time at sea. As the man of God had foretold, the next morning they found none of the monster's flesh. When the brothers came back to Brendan, they said to him: "Father abbot, what you foretold to us about that monster has come to pass." Again, the holy father said to them: "Now I will tell you another sign. A fish that escaped from a fishing net last night will be carried here tomorrow, and you will be fed from it." And so, it came to pass. The next day, when the brothers went to the shore of the island, they found a great fish there as Brendan foretold. Accordingly, they carried off as much of its flesh as they thought they would need to feed themselves. The man of God said to them: "Carefully preserve that flesh with salt, as you will need it for the time being. For tomorrow the Lord will bring about fair weather, and the storm will abate, and we will be able to sail from this place." He also instructed them to fill their vessels with spring water against future need. And he instructed them to gather herbs and roots for his own use because from the time he was ordained to the priesthood the holy man ate nothing that had the breath of life in it. When the boat was loaded with those things the man of God commissioned, they made their way in a southerly direction.

Isle of Steadfast Men. (47) As they crossed through uncharted byways of the sea, they saw an island at a distance. The man of God said to his company: "Three groups of people are on that island, one of which is composed of boys, the second of young men, the third of elders." He added: "One of our brothers will sojourn with them." The disciples asked him which of them it was who would remain with them. Because they continued to ask who it was who would stay in that place, the man of God replied: "This is he who will remain with them." And he was one of the three brothers who followed the man of God from the monastery when he was ready to board the boat.

Then they landed on the shore of that very delightful island. For the island was so remarkably flat that it seemed to be level with the face of the sea. Three orders of men were indeed there, as Brendan foretold, namely boys, young men, and elders. Just as the age groups were visibly distinct, they were also distinguished from one another by their location. For there was about a stone's-throw distance between one company and the next. And when one group stood, the other sat. Those who were standing sang this short verse: "They shall go from virtue to virtue; the God of gods shall be seen in Zion" [Ps. 83:8]. As one company, standing, sang this verse, the other got ready to rise the same way. They did so always, without any pause.

The community's prayers. (48) The first company, the boys, was clad in white garments, the second company in blue attire, the third in purple dalmatics. It was the fourth hour [10 am] when they reached the shore of the island. At the sixth hour, the three companies sang these psalms together: "May God have mercy on us and bless us" [Ps. 66:1]. And "O God, come to my assistance" [Ps. 69:2]. And "I have believed; therefore, have I spoken" [Ps. 115:1]. And they said a prayer after the psalms. Likewise, at the ninth hour [3 pm] they sang three psalms: "Out of the depths" [Ps. 129:1]. And "Behold how good" [Ps. 132.1]. And "Praise the Lord, O Jerusalem" [Ps. 147:1]. At vespers [6 pm], they sang: "A hymn, O God, becometh thee" [Ps. 64.2]. And "Bless the Lord, O my soul" [Ps. 103.1]. And "Praise the Lord, ye children" [Ps. 112.1]. After these psalms, sitting down they said the fifteen gradual psalms [Ps. 119–133]. And after all this, a bright cloud covered the island, so dense that they could see neither the island nor its inhabitants. Still, they heard voices singing and praising God until the morning vigils, and then they began the psalm: "Praise ye the Lord from the heavens" [Ps. 148:1] even to the end. After all this they sang the first twelve psalms in order from the psalter. When day began to dawn, the island was cloudless, and then they sang another six psalms: "Have mercy on me, O God" [Ps. 50:3]. And "O God, my God, to thee do I watch at break of day" [Ps. 62:2]. And "Lord, thou hast been our refuge" [Ps. 89:1]. And "All ye nations" [Ps. 46:2]. And "O God, by thy name" [Ps. 53:3]. And "I have loved" [Ps. 114:1].

Communion prayer. (49) After all this they offered up the spotless Lamb to God Almighty [celebrated Mass], and all shared communion, saying: "Take ye this sacred body and blood of our Lord and Saviour, to life everlasting."

The second monk joins the community. (50) When they had completed everything, two men from the youths' company came carrying a basket full of strange, remarkably sweet fruit, purple in colour,[55] and saying to them: "Take of the fruits of the Isle of Steadfast Men, and deliver our brother to us, and go in peace." Brendan called the aforesaid brother [who was to remain on the island] to him, and said to him: "Kiss your brothers, beloved one, and go with them who summon you. I say to you, brother, that in a happy hour did your mother beget you, since you deserve to dwell with such a company." And when he had kissed the brothers in order, Brendan said to him: "Son, be mindful of the favours God has bestowed on you in this life. Therefore, go now with them and pray for us." Bidding farewell to the brothers he followed two of the youths to the gathering place of those holy men. On his arrival, chanting this verse of the psalm, they sang: "Behold how good and how pleasant it is for brethren to dwell together in unity" [Ps. 132:1]. After that, they sang: "We praise Thee, Lord" [the *Te Deum laudamus* hymn to the Trinity] loudly; and with a kiss, he joined the community of those men.

---

55. R 125 *fructibus eis incognitis colore purpureis. Brussels* 72 and *Anglie* 147 have purple *scalts,* and *scaltis,* an unidentified fruit or berry, seemingly purple, dark red or black in hue.

Wondrous provisions. (51) After all this they left the island, sailing through byways hither and yon. When the time came to eat, the holy father instructed that some of the fruits be given to the brothers as refreshment. Taking up one cluster of the fruits, marvelling at its size, he said: "I say to you, brothers, that I cannot recall having seen or read about any clusters of fruit this large." For the fruit were the size of a large ball. The man of God called for a pitcher to be brought to him. Squeezing the juice from one fruit, he produced a pound [= twelve ounces], and, dividing it into twelve ounces, he gave one ounce to each of them.[56] And so, the brothers were refreshed for twelve days. After eating this fruit, they had the taste of honey in their mouths. When those wondrous provisions were exhausted, Brendan instructed the brothers to observe a fast for three days.

A bird brings grapes. (52) When they had finished [fasting], a bird of wondrous size flew to them carrying in its beak a branch from a tree they did not recognize and placed it in the boat before the man of God. The branch had on its tip a cluster of bright red grapes. The bird then withdrew, leaving the branch there. The man of God said to the brothers: "Beloved ones, take the meal that God has sent us through the service of this bird." Truly, those grapes were the size of crab apples. The man of God divided the grapes among the brothers for twelve days, and so they were refreshed by them all that time. That done, the saint again instructed his company to observe a three-day fast.

The isle of grapes. (53) Three days later they saw another island covered with very dense trees bearing the same yield of grapes of incredible fertility, such that the trees' branches were bent downward. No tree there was without fruit, and all the trees were of the same kind. As they set to shore there, the man of God, leaving the boat, made the rounds of the island. It had a fragrance like the scent of pomegranates.[57] Now the brothers waited in the boat until Brendan the servant of God returned. Meanwhile the wind blew toward them with the very sweet scent of the fragrant trees, which greatly refreshed them. On this island, Brendan found six flowing springs and an abundance of verdant plants. Returning to the brothers, he brought with him fruits of the island and said to them: "Leave the boat for land and pitch your tents and take of this island's fruits, for we need to refresh ourselves with them." And they were refreshed by these fruits for the forty days they were on the island. Then they boarded the boat, bearing with them as much of the produce of the island as their boat could carry.

A gryphon attacks. (54) As they were leaving the island, a certain beast called a gryphon appeared. And when the brothers saw it fly toward them, they were

---

56. Brendan would have had to make use of a second fruit to nourish his full crew, comprising the 14 original brothers, the sole remaining newcomer, and himself.

57. R 127 *malorum punicorum.*

very frightened, for it was huge and dreadful. They said to Brendan: "Help, father, for this beast hastens to devour us." He said to them: "Fear it not, for our Lord will protect us from its attack." And when the beast stretched out its talons to seize God's servants, the bird that earlier had brought them the branch with fruit suddenly rushed to meet it, and joining battle with the gryphon, it first tore out its eyes, then killed it. Indeed, the beast was as large as an ox; yet it had talons and wings like an eagle. Its body fell into the sea in front of the brothers, for they were battling high in the air. After this, the bird flew back victorious to the place from which it had come. Saved from so great a peril, they gave thanks to God, who so magnificently protected them from such a dreadful beast. After this they reached the island of the monks of Ailbhe, where, observing Christmas, they stayed the appointed time.[58] Then, after receiving a blessing from the abbot of the monastery and his monks, they sailed around the sea seeing God's wonders in the deep [Ps. 106:24].[59]

The Middle Years at Sea

The clear sea. (55) One time, as they devoutly kept the feast of St Peter the apostle [June 29], the sea appeared so transparent to them that they clearly saw everything that was in the deep as if it were at the surface. Indeed, they saw there different kinds of beasts like herds of sheep at pasture. As the brothers were terrified at the dreadful sight of such huge beasts, they beseeched the father [Brendan] to celebrate Mass silently, lest the sound of his voice provoke the monsters to attack them. The holy father answered them, saying: "I am amazed at your foolishness, you who now fear these beasts." He added: "Why did you not fear that most voracious of beasts [Casconius] on whose back you often were, sitting and singing psalms and even cooking meat? As you did not fear him then, why are you fearful now? Is not our Lord Jesus Christ God of all, who can subdue the nature of all beasts?" And when he had said that, he celebrated Mass as loudly as he could. When the beasts heard the noise of the shouting, rising to the surface of the sea they swam in a circle around the boat, yet at some distance from it. So numerous were the beasts that they could not see the sea beyond them. Yet they moved to and fro around the boat in such a way that they seemed to show reverence for the body of their Creator. When the holy man had celebrated Mass, the beasts quickly made off in different directions across the sea. Then, carried by a fair wind, it still took them eight days to cross that clear sea.

58. Rounding out their second year at sea.
59. The narrative from Chapters 55 to 62 appears to relate some of the wonders they encounter during their middle years at sea, years three through six.

The crystal column. (56) One day, while they were celebrating Masses in the boat, an extraordinarily high column appeared, which they took three days to reach. When they drew near it, they could not see its summit because of the height. This column was covered from top to bottom by such a loosely textured canopy that a boat could pass through its apertures.[60] Pondering the canopy's fine construction, they could not identify the material of which it was made. The canopy was silver in colour, and it seemed to be stronger than marble. The column was of purest crystal. Brendan said to the brothers: "Now rest from rowing and seize the netting or fittings of the canopy and that is all you need to do." The canopy stretched far out beyond the column on the sea, about 1,000 paces [a mile], and it hung from its summit down to the depths of the sea. Brendan said to the brothers: "Guide the boat through an opening in the canopy and let us carefully reflect upon the wonders of our God." When they had done this, the sea seemed to them like a sheet of very clear glass, so that they saw into the deep. Yet they could not see the column's foundations or edges. And the brightness [of the sun] shone no less below [the surface] than above. The holy man then measured one of the canopy's openings, and it was four cubits [six feet] on every side.[61] They sailed for an entire day along one side of the column, and because of its shadow they could not feel the sun's heat. The man of God made the side of the column to be 1,400 cubits [2,100 feet], and all four sides were the same length. He spent four days measuring. On the fourth day, they found a chalice made of the same material as the canopy and a paten of the same colour as the column in a window on the south side of the column. Taking hold of them, the man of God said: "Our Lord Jesus Christ has shown us these wonders so that looking on them we may glorify the might of God." He told the brothers to complete the divine office, and then to refresh their bodies. After all this, departing, they sailed north, and aided by a favourable wind, they were borne across the sea for eight days.

60. While evoking biblical images of the New Jerusalem in Apoc. 21 and of the heavenly temple in Ezek. 40–41, and possibly alluding to Prov. 18:10, "The name of the Lord is a strong tower: the just runneth to it, and shall be exalted," the description of the crystal column, with its canopy, chalice, and paten, may also be intended to evoke an altar of the later medieval era, constructed of stone, and featuring a *baldachinum* or canopy, in addition to utensils. Marie Therese Flanagan, *The Transformation of the Irish Church in the Twelfth and Thirteenth Centuries* (Woodbridge, 2010), 65–66. Brendan treats it as a holy precinct, saying the divine office there. In popular literature the column is often taken to be an iceberg, and on October 28, 2018, the National Aeronautics and Space Administration published photographs of two large "tabular" icebergs in Antarctica, remarkably rectangular in shape, that had broken off the ice shelf.

61. The aperture would be roughly six feet on a side, or eight feet across the diagonal. Taken literally, this would imply that Brendan's boat was thought to be between six and eight feet wide, and the mast removable.

The isle of the smiths. (57) When those days had run their course, they saw a very frightful island full of smiths' forges, bereft of trees and vegetation. The holy man said to his company: "Truly, brothers, I dread this island. Indeed, I do not wish to enter it, or to draw near it, yet even so the wind draws us toward it." As they were passing it at a stone's-throw distance they heard a thunderous din of blowing bellows and of hammers beating on anvils. Hearing this, the holy man armed himself by making the sign of the Lord's victory [the sign of the cross] over his entire body, saying: "Lord Jesus Christ, deliver us from this evil island." When the prayer was said, one of the island's denizens, very dreadful and shaggy, came outside as if to perform some chore. When he saw the saints of God pass by the island, he rushed back to the place from which he had come, and said: "Alas, alas, alas, for evil has befallen us!" The man of God again protected himself with the standard of the Lord's cross, saying to the brothers: "Children, hoist high the sail, and row at the same time, that you the more quickly may be able to leave this island."

The smiths attack. (58) After this, one of the smiths came out to the shore carrying in his hands tongs with a huge fiery lump of slag that he immediately hurled upon Christ's servants. Almighty God protected his own so that his attempt could do them little harm. The hurled lump went past them by a stadium's distance [600 feet], falling into the sea, and the sea began to seethe like live coal, and fumes rose from it as from a fiery furnace. When they had gone about 1,000 paces from the spot where the lump fell, then the hellish smiths came rushing to the shore each carrying a fiery mass of his own. Some of them hurled their lumps at God's servants, others cast them at their fellows. And the sons of darkness grieved that God's servants escaped their hands. So, they went back to their forges and fired them, and then the whole island appeared to be a raging, burning mass. The sea seethed like a cauldron boiling over a fire. All that day as well they heard great wailing and shouting from the island and an intolerable stench assailed their nostrils. Then the man of God, encouraging the brothers, said: "Soldiers of Christ, be strong in unfeigned faith, for truth be told, we are presently close by the mouth of the infernal pit. Therefore, keep watch, and act bravely" [1 Cor. 16:13].

Demons seize the third monk. (59) After this, to the north a high mountain appeared in the ocean, the summit of which was shrouded in clouds and smoke. Against their will, their boat was swiftly drawn to the mountain's shore by the force of the wind. The island was so high they could hardly make out its summit. For the mountain was a high wall, and its summit was entirely ablaze. The last of the three brothers who followed the man of God from his monastery [having ignored Brendan's prophesy that the voyage would not go well for him], leaving the boat for land, cried out, saying: "Woe is me, for I am carried away from you, and I cannot return to you." They left him there, hurrying to pull the boat back from the land. For they were very fearful, and said: "Have mercy on us Lord, have mercy, for we are in danger." As they looked back in fear, they saw their fellow dragged away to torments by demons, and how he was burning with a hellish fire among them. Seeing this, the brothers said among themselves: "Alas for you, wretch, that you have deserved such torment in your life." After this, aided by a favourable wind, they were carried away from that pestilential mountain and headed south. When they again looked back at the island, they saw the mountain clear of smoke and giving off flames into the sky and drawing them back again, so that the whole mountain to the sea looked like a burning funeral pyre.[62]

Paul the hermit. (60) After this, as they sailed south, a small island appeared.[63] As the brothers rowed furiously for it, Brendan said to them: "My brothers, don't tax your bodies excessively. For this coming Easter it will be seven years since you left your country." Then he said: "Now you will see a hermit on this island, Paul [a disciple of Patrick], who has lived for thirty years without any bodily nourishment, and who received food for thirty years before that through the service of a beast."[64] When he had said this to the brothers, reaching the shore they could scarcely find a place to land. For the island was rocky, and high, and circular. At its summit, there was no soil, but bare rock. The entire island was about a stadium [600 feet] across. Finally, with much effort, they barely managed to find a narrow approach through which the prow of the boat could enter, with difficulty. Then Brendan said to the brothers: "Wait here, brothers, for we may not enter the island without leave from the man of God. I alone will enter and will return to you with leave." When he had scaled the island's summit, he saw two caves facing each other and a spring near them from which the man of God drew water. The spring that gushed from the rock was soon swallowed up by it. As Brendan drew near the mouth of one cave, the old man rose to meet him from the other, saying: "Behold how good and how pleasant it is for brethren to dwell together in unity" [Ps. 132:1]. When he had said that he asked Brendan to summon the brothers from the boat.

Paul confirms Brendan's greatness. (61) When Brendan had done so, the old man kissed them, calling them by their own names. The brothers wondered not only about his spirit of prophetic knowledge, but also at the way he was clad. He was completely covered to his feet by hair from his head and other bodily hair.

---

62. At this point in the common version of the *Navigatio* Brendan and his crew meet Judas on a rock in the ocean. *R* omits the story but alludes to it at Chapter 97. A translation of the missing episode is in Appendix 1.

63. They arrive at the start of Lent, in this their final year at sea.

64. The *Book of Armagh*, fol. 18, a 2, lists a Pool (= Paul) as a member of Patrick's household. Whitley Stokes, ed. and trans., *The Tripartite Life of Patrick (Bethu Phátraic): With Other Documents Relating to that Saint* (London, 1887; repr. Wiesbaden, 1965), 2: 344–345.

And all his hair was white as snow. He had no other clothing, save for his own bodily hair. When Brendan saw such attire, he said: "Woe is me, a sinner, who wear a monk's habit and do nothing worthy of this habit, when I see a man of angelic state abiding on the earth without a habit." The old man Paul said to him: "O worthy father, to whom God has shown such great and remarkable wonders that he has shown no other saint, and you say you are not worthy to wear a monk's habit. I say to you, father, that you are greater than a monk. For a monk is fed and clothed through the work of his own hands. However, the Lord has fed and clothed you and your disciples for seven years from his hidden stores. And I, a wretch, sit here on this rock naked except for my bodily hair with which I am clad like a bird with its feathers."

Paul's link to Patrick. (62) When Brendan asked how he came to that island, from where he came, and for how long he had endured such a life, the old man replied: "I was in holy Patrick's monastery, fostered for fifty years, caring for the brothers' cemetery. One day when the dean of the monastery directed me to a grave site where I was to bury someone, a venerable elder appeared to me, saying: 'Do not dig a grave there, brother, for it is the burial place of someone else.' I said to him: 'Who are you, my lord father?' And he said: 'Why do you not recognize me? Am I not your abbot?' I said to him: 'Holy Patrick is my abbot.' And he said: 'I am he. Yesterday I left this world, and this is the place of my burial.' Showing me another place, he said: 'Dig a grave here for the other's burial. And tell no one what I say to you. Tomorrow, go to the seashore and there you will find a small boat made ready that will carry you to the place where your burial will be. There will you await the day of your death.' In the morning I went to the appointed shore and, boarding the boat that I found ready there, I began to row. When my strength finally gave out, I entrusted it to the celestial Pilot to direct. Then on the seventh day this island appeared to me. When I had landed, I thrust the boat from me into the sea, and it cut through the waters on a speedy course returning to its place. Indeed, after that, I remained here as you see. The first day I came here, a sea otter brought me a fish and a small bundle of grass, and I made a meal for myself. And so, for thirty years, the same beast brought such food to me, every third day. And through the course of so many years I suffered no hunger or thirst. Every Sunday, a little water dripped from this rock, from which I refilled my small container to meet bodily needs. After some thirty years, I came upon these two caves and this spring on which through God's grace I have lived for thirty years without other bodily sustenance. For sixty years, I have been on this island, thirty feeding on fish and thirty more living on the water from this spring. I was fifty when I left my country. I am now 150 years old.[65] As my God has promised me, I abide here in my flesh ever awaiting the day of general resurrection. Press on, then, to your own land and take with you water from this spring. You will have need of it, for you have a long season [of Lent] from now until Easter. You will observe Easter where you were wont to observe it the past six years. Then, with the blessing of your Steward, you will go to that most holy of all lands [the Promised Land of the Saints], and there you will stay for forty days. Then your God will lead you back, unharmed, to the land of your birth."

The Final Year at Sea

Final season at sea. (63) Having received a blessing from the man of God, they sailed south for the whole of Lent.[66] The water they took from the island of the man of God served as their food; they refreshed themselves with it every third day and so were invigorated as if they had taken some delicacy. Then, as the man of God had foretold, they reached the island of the Steward on Holy Saturday. And when they arrived, the Steward met them at the landing place, joyfully lifting them one at a time from the boat with his own hands. When the Holy Saturday offices were completed, he set a meal before them. After vespers, the Steward and they boarded his small boat together and they came to the island where they were wont to be at such a time, on the back of the great whale. There they remained all that night, praising God. The next day [their last Easter at sea] they celebrated Masses as was their custom. When the final Mass was said, the monster moved across the sea. Perceiving that, the brothers called out to the Lord, saying: "Hear us, O God, our saviour, who art the hope of all the ends of the earth, and in the sea afar off" [Ps. 64:6]. Brendan encouraged the brothers, saying: "Fear not, my brothers. For the stirring of this monster will not harm you but rather will assist the journey." And so, it proved to be the case. For the monster came straight to the shore of the isle of the birds. The men of God stayed there until the octave of Pentecost.

Through the great fog. (64) When that season was over, the Steward said to Brendan and his company: "Board your boat and fill the bottles from this spring. I will be your guide this time. For without me, you cannot find the Promised Land of the Saints." As they boarded, all the birds of the island said as with one

65. Paul should be 110 years old. The scribe or someone dictating to the scribe may have mistaken a *cx* for a *cl* in the exemplar. In *R*, Brendan appears to reach the isle around 521, sixty years after a date commonly given for Patrick's death, 461.

66. In their seventh and final year at sea.

voice: "May the God of our salvation prosper your journey" [Ps. 67:20]. Then they sailed to the island of the Steward, and he himself with them, and there they took on provisions for a forty-day journey. Their voyage was ever to the east, going to the aforesaid land. The Steward went always before them in a small boat, guiding them on a straight course through the sea. When forty days had passed, as evening drew near a great fog enveloped them, so that one could hardly see the other. Then the Steward said to Brendan: "Do you know what this fog is?" And he said again: "This fog shrouds the island for which you have been searching for seven years." After about an hour a great light shone around them and at once the boat rested on the shore.

The Promised Land of the Saints. (65) Then, rising from the boat, they saw a fair land full of trees bearing fruit as in the autumn season. As they made the rounds of that land night never fell on them. They took as much as they wanted from the fruits of the trees and the springs. And so they stayed for forty days exploring that land. One day, as they made the rounds of it they came upon a great river dividing the island in two. Then Brendan said to the brothers: "We cannot cross this river. And we do not know the size of this island." As they pondered these things among themselves, a young man met them who, kissing each of them, called them by their own names.[67] He said to them: "Blessed are they that dwell in thy house, O Lord; they shall praise thee for ever and ever" [Ps. 83:5]. Having said that, he said to Brendan: "Behold the land you have sought for a long time. You could not find it straightway because God wished to show you his secrets on the great sea. Accordingly, return to the land of your birth, taking with you as many fruits from this island, and precious stones, as your small boat will carry. For the day of your pilgrimage draws on when you will sleep with your fathers. After the course of many years, when a great persecution will have come upon Christians, this land will be revealed to those who come after you. So, this river that you see divides this island. And just as it appears now to you, ripe with fruit, it is ever so. And so will it remain. Moreover, night never darkens it, for Christ is its light."[68]

Heading back to Ireland. (66) Then Brendan and his company boarded their small boat, heading back the same way as before, having taken leave of their blessed Steward and the youthful herald of good tidings, and taking as many fruits and precious stones of the land as they desired. When they had passed through the fog they reached the island called the Isle of Delight or Pleasures [of Ter-

---

67. This appears to be the angelic guardian who greeted Barinthus and Ternoc in Chapter 13.

68. Plummer notes some *Navigatio* manuscripts add: "Then St Brendan said to the young man, 'Lord father, will this land ever be revealed to mankind?' And he replied, 'When the most high Creator has subjected all peoples to himself, then will this land be shown to his elect.'" *VSH* 1: 134 n4.

noc's community], staying there for three days with the brothers.[69] Then, having received a blessing from the brothers, he [Brendan] returned to his own place. The brothers [Brendan's community in Ireland] rejoiced exceedingly at the arrival of their father, glorifying God, who brought back to them their patron and comforter. The man of God, rejoicing in their affection, to comfort them told them of the wonders of God that he saw at sea.

[The common text of the *Navigatio* ends at this point.]

Brendan's Reminiscences

Satan shows them hell. (67) Among other things, he [Brendan, on his return] recounted these as well to them.[70] "One day Satan appeared to us in a shape much befitting his [evil] disposition. And he stood over the boat's sail."[71] Brendan said to him: "Why have you come to us before the due time?" He said to him: "We claim of you, in the name of the most high Christ whom you serve, that we who suffer eternal punishment derive some benefit from your arrival. For we make our wretched dwellings in the secret places of the sea." Brendan inquired as to where that place of punishment was. The demon said to him: "No man can see it and afterward live." And the demon pointed out to them the entrance to that place of punishment. However, the brothers did not see with whom the man of God was speaking, and they said: "Father, tell us to whom you are speaking in this way." He told them in turn what he heard from Satan. Then one of the brothers said to Brendan: "Father, let me see those punishments." And he allowed him to see them. When he [the brother] saw the punishments and the faces of those enduring them, he cried: "Woe to all who come to that place of torments," and

69. R 134 *ad insulam que vocabatur deliciosa vel deliciarum.* The *insula deliciosa* of Chapter 13, where Ternoc and his followers lived.

70. This is the first of two significant *cruces* in the R transition from the *Navigatio* narrative to the *Vita* narrative. This passage suggests that Brendan, on his return home, recounts additional tales of his voyage, from Chapters 67 through 76. These tales are drawn from years three through six, the middle years of his voyage, including the relaunch of Brendan's voyage at 71 after five years at sea and his subsequent adventures, all in retrospective fashion. Those incidents would have been imagined as taking place between 54 and 60 in the story line. The second *crux* is addressed at 76.

71. The narrative has Brendan speaking in the first person, saying *apparuit nobis Sathanas* (Satan appeared to us). But immediately, the story reverts again to third person narration. In *Brussels* 60, Satan appears in "an accursed and dreadful form." In *Lismore* 254, he appears "inveterate, awful, hideous, foul, hellish." In R, Brendan can see him for who he is, but the brothers cannot.

died. However, Brendan raised up the dead man, though not without much effort. After this the man of God said to the demon: "The Lord, the just judge, mighty and longsuffering [Ps. 7:12], will know which of those things that you ask for are just."

The giant girl. (68) Not far from where they left him, they saw a broad shore where they came across a dead girl whom they saw was stricken between the shoulders. Truly, she was of exceedingly great size, 100 feet in length. The holy father prayed fervently to God for her, and his prayer was heard. For he raised her up and baptized her. When she was questioned by him as to what province she was from, and what people, she replied: "I am of the dwellers in the sea, and we hope for the general resurrection." Brendan said to her: "Choose now, one or the other, whether you wish to go to your people, or to heaven." She replied in a language only the elder could comprehend: "I wish to live with my King, and to see him daily, and to dwell with the angelic spirits ever praising him." And immediately, after she had chosen Mary's part [Lk. 10:38–42], she died in peace, without struggle or suffering, and was buried in that place.

The forbidden island. (69) After this, sailing from there, they came upon a very lofty island, and they could not find a fitting place to land. After they strove for fifteen days to enter, they finally abandoned their desire. Yet they heard human voices praising God, though they could not see the singers themselves. They fell into a reverie because of the sweet singing of the spiritual song. From the cliff, a wooden writing board was thrown to them on which was written: "Do not strive to enter the island; you will find what your soul longs for.[72] Rather, return to your country, for your people yearn to see you. For this land is not promised to you. Search the scriptures, wherein it is written that in God's house there are many dwelling places" [Jn. 14:2]. So, they turned back from the island, carrying with them the writing board sent to them as a token of that joyful unseen people. And daily that writing board was read aloud by them, as if sent by God.

The deadly stream. (70) One day, as they rowed and were near dead from thirst, they saw a nearby cliff from which clear streams poured forth. The brothers said: "May we drink these waters flowing from the cliff?" The man of God said to them: "First sing hymns to hallow the water that is on display." When the waters were blessed and an alleluia sung, the streams were no longer visible. Rather, they saw a demon spewing foul fluids to kill the drinkers. Then their trial by thirst abated, and they blessed the Lord, who delivered them from death.

The tale of Brendan's second voyage. (71) After five years [at sea], the man of God returned to his own country [near Tralee in Kerry]. Hearing of his arrival, neighbours and kinsfolk came to him, asking him about his great labours. And

---

72. *Lismore* 256 has a waxed tablet, inscribed by stylus.

hearing his teaching, many followed Christ, forsaking worldly vanities.[73] There he performed many deeds of power and healings. Among other deeds of power, he converted his own father to Christ. After that he called upon Bishop Earc, and then upon Íde his foster mother. Íde received him and his disciples as if Christ and the apostles. She said to him: "My son, why did you wish to hazard that difficult labour [seeking the Promised Land of the Saints] without my guidance? You will not find the land shown to you by the Lord in the skins of dead animals, for that land is very holy, wherein human blood has not been shed. Therefore, seek out craftsmen who know how to build you a ship of wood. Perhaps in this way you may search out that land." Heeding the counsel, Brendan went to the Connacht region, for there he thought to find more fitting timbers for the work. There, with clever craftsmen, he fitted out a ship secure enough to face the trials of the sea.[74] When the craftsmen and workers asked this reward of the man of God for the labour, that he would allow them to accompany him, he granted the request for their service. When they were all ready to board, then a certain man came who held the office of herald among the people, who on bended knee humbly asked that the man of God allow him to accompany him. The holy father, yielding to his entreaties, admitted him with all the others. And the man of God gave him a tonsure, so that he might carry a symbol of religious faith on his head. Sailing in the Lord's name, they first reached Inishmore [in the Aran Islands group] where they found the saints of God, Éanna, Pupa, and Nochat, with whom they remained for a month in true affection.[75]

Rats devour the herald. (72) After this, sailing the sea from there, they saw a very lofty island where they saw rats like wild cats, that, coming to the shore, were eager to devour human flesh. Seeing them, the brothers said among themselves: "What are these beasts looking at?" Brendan replied: "They want to devour us all." The man of God then said to the herald: "Rise up and receive the body of our Lord Jesus Christ and present yourself as a sacrifice to your Lord, who offered himself in sacrifice to the Father for you, so that you may have the prize of eternal glory in return for suffering a brief hardship." He said: "I heard choirs of angels on their thrones calling to you." When the herald heard that he was promised

73. M 109: "And the man of God made them monks, and he founded many monasteries and cells across Ireland in which 3,000 monks from novices to the most senior were under him. And he made his father a monk, and his mother a consecrated widow."

74. The wooden ship favoured by Íde may be meant to suggest the Ark of the Church, a sure conveyance to paradise. Other versions give much larger crews: S² 328 gives sixty at the relaunch; *Lismore* 253 and 257 gives ninety for the first voyage, sixty for the relaunch.

75. R 136 *insulam Ayrne*. Éanna of Inishmore, his companion Pupa, who moved to Inishmore from Rome, and Nochat, who may be Ruanach of Inishmore. Ó Riain, *Dictionary*, 282, 544. *Brussels* 52 has Enda, Pupa, Ronad living on Aran. *Lismore* 257 has Enda, Pupu, Rochath.

heavenly things in exchange for earthly, making himself ready for martyrdom, he said: "O holy man of God, Brendan, by what deed do I deserve to see God today?" And taking the Viaticum of salvation, obedient to the father even unto death [Phil. 2:8], he went to the beasts. Falling on him like famished carrion flies on meat, the rats quickly devoured his flesh to the bones. They waited for the struggle to be over and buried his bones there.[76]

Burying the smith at sea. (73) Soon after, as they were sailing from there, the smith fell mortally ill and drew near death. Brendan said to him: "Brother, why do you delay going into the hands of your God? For today you have found that which you have been seeking all your life. If you wish to remain longer in the present life, we will entreat the Lord for you." The smith said to him: "I hear the Lord Jesus Christ calling me by my name." Taking the Lord's body [holy communion] as a sure guide for his journey, he fell asleep in peace. The brothers pondered where they might bury the body of the holy man. Brendan answered: "Bury him in the waves of the sea, as you do not have land at hand. For he who created all things from nothing can solidify the sea waters so that they may be made fixed for his burial." They buried him there amid the waves of the sea, and the body stood so fixed in one place that it neither sank into the depths, nor did the wave action heave him up. But he was laid as if in an earthly tomb, awaiting the final resurrection of the dead. And there he remains.

Replacing the smith. (74) After this, as they sailed through byways of the sea, a small island appeared. When they were drawing near, suddenly a multitude of demons like dwarves in shape appeared. Brendan said to his company: "Drop anchor here in the sea. For no one lands here except he who wages human wars and sheds blood." Dropping their anchor there in the sea, they stayed seven days. When that time was over, as they set about to depart, they could not weigh anchor, for it was wedged among the sea's rocks. Then the brothers, almost despairing of themselves, said: "Our smith is dead, and we have no other like him who will make an anchor for us." Brendan, trusting in the supreme Craftsman, said to his priest attendant: "You, brother, serve as our smith and accomplish all that is required, until the end of the month." Brendan blessed his hands, so he might be able to grasp the craft he lacked. Rising, the priest took the tools of the trade and soon made an excellent anchor.

The isle of the last monk. (75) They sailed from there to another very pleasant but small island where there appeared to be a tidal basin from ancient times for catching fish. When the tide ran out the marine life was left behind there. As they crossed the island, they found a stone church, and a venerable elder praying in it.

76. *Lismore* 257 and *Brussels* 53 add that his name is written in a martyrology.

And what can I say about the old man?[77] Indeed, they saw little more than living bones. The elder said to them: "Holy people of God, hastily flee this island. For there is an ancient cat here that has grown huge, having found a way to eat a great many fish."[78] They hastily returned to the ship, leaving the island. And they saw the beast swimming after them in the sea, and it had eyes as large as glass platters.[79] Then as they all applied themselves to prayer Brendan said: "Lord Jesus Christ, hold your beast in check." And immediately, another beast rose from the depths of the sea and, drawing near, fought with the other, and both sank into the depths and were not seen again. They gave thanks to God and returned to the elder, asking him about his state and from where he came. He said to them: "We came to this place, twelve men from the Isle of Ireland, seeking a place for our resurrection. Eleven have died. I alone remain, O saint of God, awaiting communion from your hands. We brought one cat in the ship with us, much beloved by us, that grew huge eating many fish, as was said. But our Lord Jesus Christ did not allow him to harm us." Then he showed them the way to the land they were seeking. And taking communion from Brendan's hands he fell asleep, joyful in the Lord, and was buried there among his fellows.

The good and holy island. (76) After this, going from there they reached a very desirable land.[80] When, drawing near it, they were seeking a suitable place to land, they heard the voice of an elder of the island saying: "O industrious pil-

77. The narrative shifts to first person, implying again that Brendan may be relating stories from earlier in his voyage, then reverts to third person.

78. *Lismore* 258 and *Brussels* 75 add that the cat was the size of a young ox or horse.

79. *Lismore* 258 and *Brussels* 75 say its eyes were the size of a brazen cauldron.

80. *R* 138 *terram valde desiderabilem.* This is a second *crux* in the transition from the *Navigatio* narrative back to the *Vita* narrative. It is tempting to see it as a variant or doubling of Brendan's meeting with Patrick's disciple Paul the hermit at Chapters 60–62 and of Brendan's subsequent arrival at the Promised Land of the Saints at 65. Both Paul and the unnamed elder are clad only in their own hair. However, at 62, Paul, who is named, directs Brendan toward the "most holy of all lands" under the Steward's guidance, where they encounter no other human being, whereas at 76, the unnamed elder is said to occupy the island. Moreover, Paul's island was a bare rocky outcrop far removed from the Promised Land of the Saints, whereas this is a "very desirable" isle. And whereas Paul does not die, the elder does, as did the hermit in the previous chapter, 75, who also was awaiting Brendan's arrival, takes communion, and dies.

While no fully satisfactory reading presents itself, this episode suggests the encounter with the man from Corcomroe whose story is narrated later, at 98. He fled the mainland to avoid family discord at a time when plural marriage was acceptable; he has lived to see Brendan ninety years later; and he calls out to Brendan's crew, takes communion from Brendan's hands, then dies. If this is the man from Corcumroe, this scene may be conceived as a final, Eden-like hermetic precinct before Brendan reaches the Aran group off the Irish coast, and home.

grims, hoping for heavenly reward, O weary toilers, endure a little while longer." As they waited a little while, again he said to them: "My brothers in Christ, behold, you see a very good and holy land undefiled by human blood nor dug up for any man's grave.[81] Therefore leave all you have in the ship except for the necessary vestments and books, and come here." Then, kissing them in turn and weeping for joy, he said: "Abide, and behold Christ's meadows and paradise amid the waves of the sea." Whereupon, seeing the wonders of God, they glorified the Lord. The elder had no clothing but was covered in his own hair, like a bird. And he spoke to them as if in the speech of angels. When they had observed the third hour [terce, 9 am], minds fixed on Christ, they in no way ventured to question him, waiting for him to speak first. He said to them: "Let each of you pray separately without addressing one another. For this land is very holy. And in a multitude of words, there shall not want sin [Prov. 10:19].[82] Also, as ancient lore has it, not without sorrow is senseless mirth begotten [Eccl. 7:5]." They replied: "We agree with you." After they prayed this way for a time, coming to them he said: "We must observe the sixth hour [sext, noon]." When they had observed it, Brendan said to him: "If God wills it, my home will be here." The elder replied: "He tests God's will, who seeks his own. Behold I dwelt here sixty years, living on the food of angels, and when I came to this place, almost all my allotted time was gone. Then Christ my lord told me that you would come to this holy island, and so I endured here thirty years more in my old age. Indeed, today I must enter [eternal] life. You, however, go to the land of your birth after the ninth hour [none, 3 pm]. Proclaim to your Irish people all that pertains to their souls' salvation. Through you will the people's evil deeds be shorn away. For my God told me this very hour that at the end of time your remains will be brought to this island with your religious community, and with the anchor marvellously wrought by unlearned hands. This will take place seven years before the Last Judgment."[83] After this, when they had observed the ninth hour, a bird came to them that put a half loaf of bread before each of them and a portion of fish. They ate of it, giv-

---

81. *Lismore* 259 and *Brussels* 76 have Brendan finding the Land of Promise at this point, and say it is no place to bury sinners or evil men.

82. Notably, the man from Corcumroe flees his wives' chatter when it leads to discord.

83. At the time of an expected inundation of Ireland prior to the Great Tribulation, described in Mt. 24: 21–25, Mk. 13, Lk. 21, Apoc. 7–16, that precedes Judgment Day. In the *Book of Armagh*, St Patrick is said to have asked God to cause the sea to flood Ireland seven years before the day of judgment, to spare the Irish the horrors of the tribulation. See John Carey, "Saint Patrick, the Druids, and the End of the World," *History of Religions* 36, no. 1 (1996): 42–53, at 47–48. The *Life of Colum of Terryglass* has Colum's people migrating in the latter times "to the Land of Promise in the sea." Ó Riain, *Four Tipperary Saints*, 15.

ing thanks together to the bestower. Then the holy elder, taking the Viaticum of salvation, died, and was buried there in peace.[84]

Brendan's Missions

Reaching Ireland. (77) After two years [following the relaunch] they returned to the Isle of Inisheer [in the Aran Islands].[85] There, lodged by the brothers with great joy, they gave an orderly account of what they had seen. When they [the Aran monks] heard this, they wept for joy and pleaded with Brendan, saying: "Abide with us. For behold, this land is in your hand." To which he replied: "My resurrection is not here." When they had stayed there a month, leaving his marvellous cup and anchor there, they came to Ireland, landing at Inishdadroum Island [Inis da droma in Clare] near the town of Limerick.[86] Fasting there for seven days without human nourishment, seven of them died and were buried there.

The cursed river. (78) At one time, Brendan sent two of his disciples to the fishers of the river Fergus [in Clare], to provide fish for the brothers' use. When they refused, through God's just judgment it came to pass that the river remained barren. This same wonder was done to many waters for the same reason.

Curing Bryoss. (79) At another time, he came to the Clyach region [in Tipperary] and stayed the night there in Bryoss, a renowned place.[87] And coming to him the people there said: "This place is greatly afflicted, for it begets fleas as numerous as the sand of the sea." Then the man of God, taking pity on them, prayed, saying: "Lord, deliver them who have received us in your name from this affliction." And so, it came to pass.

Cursing settlements. (80) At his word the settlements of fifty kings were vacated because their residents wronged the holy man, and they remain deserted.[88]

The drowned youth. (81) When he had entrusted his ship to the care of a boy at the island of Inishdadroum and, as the tide came in, the boy's brother, mut-

---

84. This is the end of the sequence of tales from Brendan's voyage that *R* appears to recount in retrospect. The story now has Brendan sailing back to his homeland.

85. *R* 140 *insulam Ayrne Airthir.*

86. *R* 140 *insula Druma*; *M* 110 *de Trumma*; *S²* 329 *de Druma*. The marvellous cup appears to be Earc's cup from Chapter 96.

87. *R* 140 *Bry Oss*. The hill of the stag, in Tipperary. *M* 110 places the settlement of Briuys in the Cliach region near Sliabh Muice/Slievenamuck, in Tipperary. *Anglie* 152 has Elioch, likely for Cliach. *Brussels* 78 gives Inber Ais in Cliach as the location.

88. *Brussels* 78: At Bri Oiss in Cliach.

tering, feared lest the boy with the boat perish, Brendan replied: "If you care to have greater compassion for him than I, go, take his place and watch over the ship." When he went to help his brother, the sea came in on all sides and he was drowned in the raging waters. But for the boy, the sea was like a wall on the right and left, as it once was for Moses and his people at the Red Sea [Ex. 14:21–30].

Íde counsels Brendan to go abroad. (82) However, Brendan felt a qualm of remorse for the death of the drowned youth, and consulting all the holy men of Ireland he sought their advice on a form of penance from the scriptures.[89] When he had come to his nurse Íde the virgin and had told her of the youth's death, the virgin of Christ said to him: "You must go to a foreign land to teach others, and gain souls for Christ."

Gildas tests Brendan. (83) Heeding his nurse's counsel, he went to Britain.[90] Hearing of the repute of the most holy Gildas, a man of great power, he hastened to visit him, taking with him men of religion.[91] When they had come to Britain, and the Holy Spirit had revealed their arrival to Gildas, he said: "Make ready a meal. For a holy and hardworking people of God are about to come to us. Indeed, they are at hand, and you will see the apostle Peter, as it were, restored in the flesh, a very great, industrious abbot." At the time, it was winter. When they had come to the gate of the town where the man of God [Gildas] was, then the holy man told his gatekeeper to shut up the entrance to the town with seven iron bars, wishing to test the steadfastness of their perseverance. So, they spent the night under the open sky praising God, and while deep snow covered the entire land, even so, it did not touch them. The gatekeeper, rising in the morning, addressed them from the town wall, saying: "Come to the gate and let your merits open it for you." Then Brendan instructed his attendant Chamath to open the entrance.[92] Carrying out the order immediately, he went to the gate and when he stretched out his hand toward the entrance the seven iron seals placed there beforehand fell away and were not seen again. After this they came to the shrine in the town, which was shut with three locks. Because they had no keys to open it, Brendan placed his hands on the leaves of the doors of the church, and said: "Mother Church of Christ, open your doors to us." When this was said, those seals were never seen again.

89. *M* 111 adds: "They told him: 'Go to God's holy prophet Íde, your nurse, and she will tell you what it behooves you to do.'"

90. *R* 141 *ad Britanniam.*

91. Gildas, ca. 500–570, a British monk who was associated with David, bishop of Mynyw in Wales, and with Cadoc, abbot of Llancarfan. Gildas wrote *De Excidio et Conquestu Britanniae* (On the Ruin and Conquest of Britain). For Gildas, see *AI* 74–75 and *AU* 84–85, 88–89. *M* 111 and *Brussels* 81 say it took Brendan three years to get there.

92. In *M* 112 and *S²* 330 the attendant is Talmach.

Miracles at Mass. (84) Then the minister of the church, at Gildas' command, said to Brendan: "Holy man of God, Brendan, offer up the body of our Lord Jesus." For an altar had been made ready, with a book written in Greek.[93] Accordingly, opening the book, Brendan said: "Christ, let your writings be open to us! For those who believe in you, all things are possible." And instantly those Greek writings were unveiled to him as if they were Latin.[94] When [the consecration at] Mass was concluded, Gildas was called with the people to receive the sacrament [the Eucharist]. As Gildas drew near to receive the Lord's body he saw a human finger on the paten and blood in the chalice.[95] Fearing God's vengeance upon himself, Gildas said: "How have I deserved that God's judgment should come upon me?" Brendan said to him: "My hand will shield your head from vengeance. For you put strangers to the test. Now it is time to forgive you." As Brendan blessed the altar again, the Lord's body appeared on the paten [in the form of consecrated bread], and wine in the chalice, with water. After everyone had seen the Lord's body, he stayed there three days and nights.

Domesticating lions. (85) When Brendan told him the purpose of his journey, that he wanted to do salutary penance for the drowned man, Gildas replied: "I am not a fit judge for your fault. Yet I say to you on behalf of our Lord Jesus Christ, that you should go into the wilderness near here, where a lion and lioness live that attack our people daily."[96] Hearing the counsel of saving penance, Brendan gladly complied and went into the wilderness with his attendant Calmach.[97] When they had reached the beasts' place at noon, they found the she-lion asleep. Then Brendan said to his disciple: "Rouse this beast from sleep." When he did so, the lioness, being roused in the lair in such an unaccustomed fashion, gave out a great roar. Then the lion immediately rushed to her roar. And the man of God commanded the lions to hasten with him into the town. O wonderful power of God Almighty, who made savage lions so heed the man's voice that they followed him into the town just as household dogs are wont to follow their masters. Although the townsfolk expected they would be killed, they saw them return in good health, and the lions following in their tracks, one after the other. Then the people mounted their horses and chariots and fled to a safe place, fearing the

---

93. *R* 141 *librum grecis conscriptum literis.* S^2 330: a missal written in Greek. Possibly a *Liber Usualis* containing chants for the Mass, the divine office, and various rituals.

94. S^2 330 adds: "For divine power (*uirtus*) ... opened the meaning to him, and he read the Greek as if it were Latin."

95. *M* 112 *carnem crudam ... et sanguinem*, raw flesh and blood.

96. *M* 113 adds: "And God [will] empower you to expel them that ... through this you may know he has pardoned the fault that brought you here."

97. *M* 113 and S^2 330: Talmach, as at Chapter 83, suggesting that the Chamath and Calmach of *R* are the same person.

lions' savagery because it often befell them. The man of God ordered the lions not to molest the people but rather defend them with all their strength, which the lions did. For they fed among them like household dogs, and like shepherds they guarded their herds. When Gildas saw this, fearing Brendan, he said: "Man of God, accept me as your disciple and obedient monk for all time. Also, let your judgment be in God's hand. Yet I offer this counsel and I pray that it may please you: Stay here and rule this people and watch over this place." Brendan said to him: "What is the present world to me?"[98] And declining what was offered, he and his company then left with the blessing of the man of God, although everyone wept, for they all cherished him like a father.

Brigit's sanctity. (86) After that he came to Auerech, an island in Britain, and founded a church there, intending to remain there until his death.[99] However one day, as he prayed alone on a high cliff by the sea, he saw two beasts rise from the depths of the ocean, and battle fiercely with each other. As one turned to flee, it said in a human voice to its pursuer: "I adjure you in the name of Brigit the Irish virgin to let me go." As soon as that was said, the pursuing monster left off chasing the other. After hearing these beasts' discourse, the man of God returned to the brothers, saying: "Let us rise up quickly and return to Ireland to call on Brigit."[100] When they reached Ireland, he reported to Brigit what he heard from the beasts, saying: "O Brigit, how did you deserve that the sea monster begged for your service when you were physically absent? For I was there and was ignored." She replied: "I will make known to you, father, the true reason for this. From the day I once gave myself into my Christ's hands, I have never turned my mind to worldly things. You however are often put to the test, and the world chases after you."

Heresy in Britain. (87) Brendan went to Britain again and founded a church there, Bledach, in the Heth region [on the Isle of Tiree, off the coast of Scotland], where he did many deeds of power.[101] He also saw there a wondrous vision, which he did not reveal to the brothers, save that Britain would embrace a most grievous heresy before the Last Judgment.

The Connacht king's horses. (88) After he saw that vision, arising quickly, he came to Ireland. Going into the Connacht region, he lived on an island, Inchiquin

98. *M* 113 has Brendan say, "I will not tarry here, for my resurrection will be in Ireland."

99. *M* 113: Ailech; *Brussels* 83: Ailec. Seemingly Eileach an Naiomh, a small island south of Mull near the Scottish mainland.

100. In *M* 114, the beast being pursued first appeals to "Patrick, archbishop of the Irish," then to Brendan, and finally to Brigit, with success.

101. *M* 113 refers only to the Heth region. *Brussels* 84 has Bleit in the district of Letha. *S²* 330 has Brendan founding two monasteries in Britain, one on the isle of Ailech, the other at Bledua in the Ethica region. Plummer, *VSH* 1: xxxvi–xxxvii n5, sees possible confusion between Tir Etha in Tiree, and Tir Letha in Armorica, Brittany.

Island [Inis maca Cuind at Lough Corrib in Galway], where two horses of the king of the region were pastured, which Brendan employed for the brothers' use.[102] When the haughty king, Áed mac Echach, heard of this, he was indignant and said: "I will go and slay that man who put my horses to work in so servile a manner."[103] And after uttering that arrogant speech he sought to carry out his wicked deed. Leaping up in a rage, he came to the island's harbour intending to land. But a violent wind hindered him for three days and nights. Then, as the angry king waited for fair weather, the Lord appeared in a dream saying: "Take heed that you do no harm to this Christian man. Otherwise, you will surely die." Terrified by the dreadful vision, he gave the island with the horses to the man of God.

Raising a slain monk. (89) At that time Brendan sent five of his company to the isle of Inishdadroum to serve God there. As they dwelt together, it chanced that one killed another by smiting him on the head with a hatchet. As soon as he was killed, the brothers sent messengers to Brendan to advise him of the brother's death. Brendan said to them: "Return and say to the dead one: 'Rise quickly and awake. Brendan summons you.'" When the brothers did so, the one who was dead arose at once and came with them to Connacht, bearing the hatchet in his head. When he had come to the man of God, he [Brendan] said to him: "Choose now one or the other, whether you wish to live longer here, or to go now to heaven." Whereupon, happy to have the choice, he chose heaven, and spurned the fleeting world. He died on the isle of Inchiquin, and for that reason it is known there to this day as Tollcind's grave.[104]

Freeing a man from bondage. (90) At another time the man of God went to a neighbouring plain on the island where a man met him who, weeping, fell at his feet, saying: "Have pity on me, man of God, for I am subject to a most heavy burden of bondage to this king." The merciful father, pitying the man, dug in the earth with his staff and lifted a mass of gold from the hole, and bestowing it on the poor man, said: "Tell no one from whom you received this gold, but go to the king and give it to him for your freedom and that of your kin." The poor man, giving thanks for so great a gift, went away and surrendered it to the king for his deliverance. But because the Lord's lamp cannot be put under a bushel basket [Mt. 5:15], the poor man was unable to conceal God's kindness. Rather, he made

---

102. *R* 143 *Maccu Chuind*; *M* 114 *Hynis Meic I Chuind*. *S²* 330 and *Brussels* 84 name the location as Loch Oirbsen (Lough Corrib in Galway). *M* 115 adds that Bishop Maoineann (see Chapter 91) was with Brendan there.

103. King of Connacht (d. 578). *AI* 76–77.

104. *R* 144 *sepulcrum in Tollcind*. From Irish "toll chuind" (split or pierced head). *M* 115 adds: *sepulchrum eius scotice dicitur Lebaydh in Toll-Chynd, id est Lectus Perforati Capitis* (his grave was called in Irish "Lebaydh in Toll-Chynd," that is, the resting-place of the pierced head).

known to the king from whom he received that sum. Hearing of the miracle wrought in the finding of the gold, the king said: "Christ's gold is not mine to keep but belongs to his servants. I will grant you freedom without payment; go where you will." Freed from bondage, lest he be ungrateful to his deliverer, the man returned to Brendan, acknowledging his kindness.[105]

Founding Clonfert. (91) When the man of God was seventy-seven years old, he founded a church at Clonfert [Cluain Ferta in Galway], saying: "Here will I dwell forever" [Ps. 131:14].[106] After he had been there for a time the boy Senan died, whom he had brought with him from Britain. Then Brendan, grieving the death of his disciple, said to a British bishop, Maoineann, who likewise had come with him from Britain: "Place my staff over the boy." When the order was carried out, the boy, who had died three days earlier, arose hale and whole.[107]

Íde's marvellous visit. (92) In those days Íde, grieving the absence of Brendan her foster child, said: "Oh if only I could see holy Brendan my beloved foster child with my eyes, and hear his voice with my ears, and take the body of my Lord Jesus Christ from his hands this very night of my Lord's Nativity!" And her prayer was heard. For that chosen night like another prophet Habakkuk [Dan. 14:32–38] she was lifted high in the air by an angel and around the first watch of the night [after sunset] was marvellously transported to Clonfert [from Killeedy]. Perceiving this in the spirit, Brendan, rising quickly, went to meet his nurse.[108] And where the virgin's feet set down a stone was placed as a sign of the wonder. And Brendan said: "This will be the burial place of the lepers." And so, it came to pass. Then, having taken the Lord's body from Brendan's hand, carried aloft by the angel she was brought back in the same way through the air, a seven-day journey, in the blink of an eye.[109]

Ciar quenches a fire. (93) At another time, making the rounds of Munster, he came to a region, Múscraige Tire [east of Lough Derg in Tipperary],[110] where a

---

105. S^2 330 adds, in an incident that is found in no other Latin Life: "[Then Brendan] said to the brothers: 'We must go to the country of the Uí Maine [in Connacht]. For that land has need of our ministry. There our remains must lie. For I heard an angel there fighting in my name. Therefore, in our Redeemer's name let us be of use to him.'" This incident appears as well in the Brussels Irish Life (*Brussels*, 85). S^2 330–331 goes on to say that Áed mac Echach, the king of Connacht, battled Diarmait mac Cerbaill, the high king of Ireland, that year (561) at Cúl Dreimne, and was victorious.

106. Implying a date of ca. 563 for the founding of Clonfert. Maoineann, its first bishop, died in 572. *AU* 86–87.

107. M 116 adds that Senan was despatched, "his health restored," back to his native Britain.

108. M 116 adds that Brendan brings her communion.

109. The distance is about 86 miles. M 117 makes it a three-day journey, implying a much longer walking day, or travel on horseback.

110. M 117 *Muscray Thire.*

wondrous fire rose from the very ground that gave off sulphurous flame and a dreadful stench up to the sky. And the man of God said to the people: "Behold, the fire of hell." For such was its fury that for three years all the people with much water were unable to extinguish it. "Fast for three days and pray to God that he may douse the fire," the holy man told them. As they fasted, he added this, saying: "Go, everyone, to your holy Ciar [of Kilkeary in Tipperary], that she may pray for you.[111] For she will be granted the power by the Lord to put out this fire." And when they all went to her and humbly asked her to quench the great evil, that very hour, with her praying, the fire was put out and appeared no more. Because the most holy virgin had subdued the fire of fleshly appetite in herself, therefore with God she deserved to quench the raging, material flame of that fire among the people.

Brendan of Birr. (94) After this, Brendan came to the town of Birr [in Offaly] to visit another Brendan, where that man of God was staying in heavenly contemplation. He arrived there with his company during Lent, more particularly on Good Friday. Since the man of God [Brendan of Birr] was distressed at the guests' arrival because he had no other food but meat to set before them, moved by charity, he arranged to set out what he had for them, that is, salt pork, that they might eat.[112] Indeed, the guests, observing the gospel ideal, ate what was set out, asking no questions for conscience' sake [1 Cor. 10:25–33]. As they all with thanksgiving partook of the food that was brought in fear and love of God, one lay associate, on the contrary, turning away from the brotherly rule, spitting out the bacon, ate only bread in front of everyone. The next day the brothers' scraps of meat seemed to be loaves of pure wheat, but conversely the remains of [the associate's] bread appeared to be raw flesh, swarming with worms.[113] Brendan said to him: "This year, in the forest, you will eat the roasted flesh of a beast of burden nursing its foal.[114] At that very hour your throat will be slit by enemies." And it came to pass as the man of God said.[115]

King Diarmait. (95) When Diarmait son of Cerbaill ruled in Ireland, Brendan went to the northern regions of the country, wishing to visit the faithful living

111. R 145 *Keram;* M 117 *Thyar.* For Ciar of Kilkeary, see Ó Riain, *Dictionary,* 167–168.

112. Plummer, *VSH* 1: cxiv, notes that customarily in Irish monasteries, "The ordinary fasts were relaxed in honour of visitors."

113. The *Life of St Brigit* features an episode in which two nuns refuse to eat meat hospitably set out for them by St Ibar during the Lenten fast and are reproached for it. Richard Sharpe, *Medieval Irish Saints' Lives: An Introduction to Vitae Sanctorum Hiberniae* (Oxford, 1991), 171.

114. See Lev. 22:26–28.

115. The *Life of Ciarán of Seirkieran* has a similar incident featuring Ciarán, Brendan, and Ciarán of Clonmacnoise, in which a monk, Mac Conghail, refuses to eat with the holy men

there.[116] And then King Diarmait had a dream of two angels lifting the golden chain from his neck and handing it to another man of mature years set among many elders. Brendan came the next day to pay his respects to the king. When the king had seen him, he said: "Truly, this is the man of whom I spoke to you yesterday, whom I saw in a dream being given the golden torque from my neck." Then the king's sages said to him: "Your [pre-Christian] kingdom, O king, is at an end, and it will be given to holy men of the church. And this is indeed the one to whom your kingdom is given by God and his angels."[117] The dream was reported to blessed Brendan, and how the sages interpreted its meaning to the king, and he said: "This saying is true, that for those who revere God, all things work together unto good [Rom. 8:28]. 'Seek ye first the kingdom of God,' said the Saviour, 'and all these things shall be added unto you'" [Mt. 6:33].[118]

Earc's lost cup. (96) One time, when the man of God and his company were lodged with a head of a household it happened that one of the brothers forgot his shoes there. When the brother went back and found the shoes the brothers praised God on his return because he recovered them whole, in perfect repair. Then Brendan said to the brothers: "O brothers, praise the Lord, and tell no one what I say to you while I remain in this life. For our elder, Bishop Earc, at one time entrusted me with a certain bronze cup from which he used to drink, charging that I should carefully keep it safe. We left that cup on the back of the sea monster that first Easter when the brothers fled to the boat as the beast stirred, abandoning their equipment there. I grieved the cup's loss, fearing that I had transgressed the elder's instruction. The following Easter, when we arrived at the same place, we found our cup where we left it, unblemished. I brought this cup with me and returned it to Earc. When the holy father heard of the loss of the cup and of its marvellous rediscovery, weeping, he said: 'O bronze cup, how have I deserved that so great a wonder be done through you? For henceforth you will be so dearly cherished, that you will remain an example to posterity.' And so, it came to pass."

and spurns a piece of cooked bacon. Ciarán of Seirkieran tells the monk that he will discard his habit and eat meat during Lent, a sin, and will be decapitated by enemies that very day, and will not see heaven. Pádraig Ó Riain, trans., *Four Offaly Saints* (Dublin, 2018), 46; *VSH* 1: 229–230. The *Life of Ruadhán of Lorrha* contains a similar *topos*. Ó Riain, *Four Tipperary Saints*, 83.

116. Diarmait mac Cerbaill (r. ca. 544 to 565), "the pivotal king in Tara tradition," whose reign "marks the transition from pagan to Christian kingship." Ann Dooley and Harry Roe, *Tales of the Elders of Ireland: Accallam na Senórach* (Oxford, 1999), xx. *M* 117 says that Diarmait ruled from Tara in Meath. The great-grandson of Niall Noígiallach, his family lived around Slane, north of Tara. Byrne, *Irish Kings*, 93.

117. *M* 117 adds: "And this holy man will rule over a great *paruchia* in Ireland."

118. *M* 118 adds: "And King Diarmait paid homage to St Brendan. For he was a staunchly just (*iusti tenax*) Catholic king."

Meeting Judas. (97) One winter day as the man of God walked with the brothers a storm of snow and hail fell on them, so that they could scarcely move forward. Indeed, snow covered the earth. The brothers, thinking in human fashion, said to one another: "Is the pain of Hell worse than this cold?" Hearing this, Brendan said: "Listen, brothers, to what I say to you: During my travels, one day we heard great weeping and lamentation on the sea, such that that each of our souls shuddered. And we sailed close to it, wanting to know the cause of the lamentation. We scanned the open face of the sea and on it we caught sight of a solitary rock from which the miserable and mournful voice came. For the sea rose over the rock on all sides, and from the east it cast a burning torrent and from the west an icy torrent of intolerable cold. So was proved the word of Job that: In their punishment they will go from the cool waters, to scorching heat [Job 24:19]. Asked who it was who gave out such a doleful cry, he who was suffering so replied: 'I am Judas Iscariot, the betrayer of Christ. Here I await resurrection, until the day of the great judgment.' Then we all wept, pitying his misery." After he [Brendan] related this, he continued, saying: "Brothers, is not that misery of Judas greater than this chilly hardship that we endure today?"[119]

The man from Corcumroe. (98) Another time, when the man of God and his company had stayed in a very pleasant and beautiful place, the brothers said to him: "No one could leave this lovely land for Christ's sake." And he said to them: "Listen to this. There was a very wealthy man in the territory of Corcumroe [in Clare] who had two wives, according to the law at that time.[120] This man walked in God's commandments, giving charity, and tithing in his honour. And the wives said to him: 'How long will you live with us like this?'[121] He replied: 'Until discord breaks out between you. For the Lord Jesus Christ is driven away from peo-

119. For a translation of the Judas Episode in the common version of the *Navigatio*, see Appendix 1. In an unorthodox passage, it has Brendan championing a respite from punishment. So does *M* 118: "One day as St Brendan was taking a walk, heavy snow and hail and a biting wind fell upon them on the way. And some of the brothers said to St Brendan: 'Father, the cold of hell can't be worse than this cold storm.' To whom he replied: 'Brothers, you are talking like simpletons. One Sunday at sea, we saw Judas, the betrayer of the Lord, dreadfully wailing and lamenting atop a rough and slippery rock, which at times was swallowed by waves and at other times was barely above the sea. From the east a burning flood and from the west another of glacial cold came over the rock, and soaked Judas dreadfully. And yet this great torment seemed to him to be a respite. For on Sundays through the mercy of God this place is given to him as a place of rest. What then is it like to be in hell?' Hearing these words, the brothers besought almighty God to ease his miseries." *R* avoids controversy, making no mention of Judas enjoying a Sunday respite.

120. *R* 148 *Corcumruad*. This may be the elder from Chapter 76 who meets Brendan after spending many years on his remote island.

121. *Anglie* 152 adds: "not being married."

ple by discord, and then the demons draw near to them.' Indeed, after a little time, hearing them quarrel, he arose, counselled by the Spirit, and going alone to the sea at Ath Lagen [in Clare] near Aran and finding a boat there made ready by God, he boarded and was carried to an island far removed from people where he remained, until he called out to us and received the Eucharist from my hand. And this man was clothed in the hair of his body, in the manner of a bird. Blessed will he be who forsakes this world, as that man did."

The island on columns. (99) One day when Brendan was walking with his company in the wilderness of Gaul, and a great wind was blowing, one of the brothers said: "We fear that these huge trees will fall on us and kill us." Hearing this, Brendan said: "Listen to me, brothers. One night, when we were at sea, I alone was keeping watch as the others slept. While I was praying, I saw an island in the sea which was held up by four very tall columns, and ships were entering beneath them. For there were three ships there at the same time, tied up with cables, and the wind was rocking them. See then that God, who held up the island on four columns, can deliver us today from harm from these trees."

Redeeming Colmán after death. (100) Another time one of the brothers said to another in the presence of the man of God: "Can the sins of the dead be redeemed by their living friends?" The holy father, hearing the conversation, said: "Listen to me, brothers. One night when we were on the great sea and had given up our bodies to sleep except for one who kept watch, our watchman saw an exceedingly dreadful and dark cloud coming toward him from the far reaches of the west. Smitten by both fear and dread at the same time, he hastened to rouse me saying: 'Wake up, father, and see the wondrous cloud and hear the mournful voice. For in its midst the figure of a very dark man appears, as black as charcoal or a raven.' As he drew near the ship, he made great lament, saying to me: 'I implore you in the name of Jesus Christ that you entreat the Lord for me today and tomorrow and Sunday after tomorrow, for I am the spirit of a sinner.' That said, he went away. Then we all got up and pleaded to the Lord for him. Three days later he came again, his body was the colour of a hyacinth [violet blue], and he made less sorrowful lament. Once more, he earnestly begged that we pray to the Lord again for three more days on his behalf. Having said that, he immediately went away. Again, we urged divine clemency for him. Then, toward the end of the week, he appeared in a pale cloud, and his body seemed to shine like the sun. And we heard what seemed like seven other voices like his in that pale cloud. Then he said to us: 'I thank my God and yours, for he had mercy on me on account of your prayers, and now calls me to a heavenly dwelling.' I said to him: 'What is your name?' 'Colmán the monk,' he replied to him,[122] 'who was a most iras-

---

122. The author or copyist has forgotten that Brendan is speaking in the first person. This Colmán is not Colmán of Cloyne (Chapter 8), who died after Brendan.

cible and disruptive brother.' After blessing the brothers, he hastened to heaven. By this, brothers, it is evident that the prayer of the living greatly assists the dead."[123]

Saving Connacht from war. (101) Another time the kings of Munster came in great numbers and strength to ravage the land of Connacht. At the request of the people of Connacht, Brendan came to meet the kings, to frustrate their design. But the pleas of the man of God were not heard. For they refused to understand that they might do well [Ps. 35(36):4]. But divine goodness heard what mortal savagery did not heed. For the man of God prayed as the holy prophet Elisha did rousing himself in prayer against the proud Assyrians [4 Kings 6:15–18], and the sinners could not move forward from the place where they stood but were whirled about in circles marching around the same place, their giddy passion led astray. Because vexation at last brings reflection and introspection, turning away from their wicked design they said to one another: "What we are attempting is foolish. For who can resist or oppose the will of the living God? Let us go back to our own country and leave Connacht at this time." They returned home, frustrated in their desire. The man of God then went back to his company, giving thanks to God Almighty who thus thwarted the kings' iniquity.

And as he walked on the road, a man who was mute from his mother's womb was presented to him. When he blessed his tongue in the name of the Lord, the mute man immediately spoke, and the bystanders were astonished.

Brendan foresees his death. (102) After this the holy father came to visit his sister Brígh, who lived at Annaghdown.[124] When he was there, one Sunday after the solemnities of Mass, he said to the brothers: "Today my Lord summons me to eternal life. But you, when I am dead, carry my body from here to my community of Clonfert. For God's merciful help will be there for all time. One of you shall carry my body in a chariot so that the people see no great lamentation. Also, a one-eyed lay person, Curryn mac Setni, will meet the person carrying my body, and will say to the brother: 'What are you carrying, hidden in the chariot?' Coming near, he will see my body in the chariot and will say in a dreadful voice: 'Give up this holy man of God. For here will your resurrection be, holy man of God.'

123. There is a similar story in Bernard of Clairvaux's *Life of St Malachy*, where the saint prays for his dead sister. Flanagan, *Transformation*, 216–217.

124. R 149 *Enach Duyn*, on Lough Corrib in Galway. M 119 adds that Brígh ruled Annaghdown monastery in Connacht in the territory of the Uí Briúin, under Brendan's care. S² 331 adds that Brendan tells her that she will not die at Annaghdown but in her own country, the *Trageorum terra* among the Ciarraighe in Kerry, and advises her to go there so that the people may benefit from God's compassion through her. Annaghdown is to be a place for male clerics, not women. Brendan also tells her that he will die on Sunday, three days hence. After saying Mass, Brendan asks them to pray for him. Brígh then says, "What do you fear, father?" Brendan answers, "I fear that I am to journey alone, that the way will be dark, I fear an unknown country, the presence of the King, the Judge's sentence."

Then the charioteer, stretching out his hand to a nearby clod of earth, will find a mass of gold there. And he will say to him: 'Take this gold and let us go our desired way.' He will say: 'I will not allow it, nor will I take your gold.' And, again, the brother will say to him: 'You shall rule over your people, and in due course your seed [will rule] after you.' Moreover, the brother will say as a token of proof that he [Curryn] pondered that day how he might gain lordship among his brothers. Then he will allow him to go in peace. And the brother will bless him for this."

Brendan dies. (103) When the true seer had said all this, for all things to come were present to him as if in a divine mirror, he bade farewell to the brothers and to his sister who was called Brígh, that is, the virtuous one. As he tried to enter the house he fell across the threshold, saying: "Into thy hands, Lord, I commend my spirit. Thou hast redeemed me, O Lord, the God of truth" [Ps. 30:6]. And then, having uttered these words in the hands of his holy disciples, the proven perfect imitator of Christ departed to heaven at the age of ninety-three, as the angels whose teaching he kept on earth rejoiced.

Columba of Iona foresees Brendan's death. (104) Indeed, what is read in the *Life of Columba the Abbot* should not go unmentioned here. Just as Christ announced Lazarus' death to the apostles [Jn. 11:11], so Columba in the spirit foretold Brendan's death to his disciples. For he saw his soul carried to the heavens amid the angelic choirs. And so, he instructed the brothers to celebrate the solemnities of Mass in his honour.[125]

Brendan's burial at Clonfert. (105) The next day his blessed body was placed in his chariot as he himself had arranged earlier, and a single charioteer with him on the way so as not to be held back by the residents of the region.[126] As the man of God had said earlier, he met a lay person, Curryn, on the way, who, fulfilling all that Brendan had foretold, in the end finally gave leave for the body to be carried to Clonfert. With his permission, the charioteer carried his holy charge to the appointed place without further hindrance. And there he was buried with honour on May 16 in the reign of our Lord Jesus Christ, who with the Father and the Holy Spirit lives and reigns, God, for ever and ever. Amen.

[The *R* account of the *Vita Sancti Brendani* ends here.]

---

125. In the *Life of St Columba*, III, 11, he orders Mass celebrated for Brendan of Birr. Adomnán, *Life of St Columba*, trans. Richard Sharpe (London, 1995), 214.
126. *M* 121 says it was a three-day journey to Clonfert from Annaghdown.

Brendan's Prayer

Part I

1. Introduction

Brendan the monk fashioned this prayer from the word of God through Michael the archangel of God when he crossed the seven seas seeking the promised land, and this prayer was given to him after seven paschal seasons as he observed Easter at sea for seven successive years.[1]

Truly, I say that whoever shall chant this prayer for himself or for his friend, whether living or dead, his sins will be remitted, and he will be spared future punishments. If this prayer is chanted ten times on bended knees, or prostrate, it has the worth of a hundred readings of the psalter, a hundred Masses and a hundred prayers for the dead. The counsel of the Holy Spirit taught Brendan this prayer. This is certain.

2. Invocation of Christ

In the name of the Father, and of the Son and of the Holy Spirit. Amen.

Through your holy annunciation, Lord Jesus Christ, spare me.

Through your holy conception, Lord Jesus Christ, spare me.

Through your holy nativity, Lord Jesus Christ, spare me.

Through your holy epiphany, Lord Jesus Christ, spare me.

---

1. *Brussels* 198–199 (*LIS* 2: 89): "'Search and peruse the divine scriptures [Michael the archangel tells Brendan], and make a collected prayer out of them, which may preserve and protect the men of the world from hell and its many pains.' Brendan then while in his boat made the celebrated prayer, and Michael the archangel blessed the prayer of Brendan, and said that it should be recited twelve times in a day for the soul of every sinner, and twelve genuflexions after each recitation, and a *Pater noster* on the completion of each course. And there is no sin so great, whether of living or dead, but shall receive remission, if only this be done for him" (Plummer's translation).

Through your holy passion, Lord Jesus Christ, spare me.

Through your most conscientious abstinence, Lord Jesus Christ, spare me.

Through your holy cross, Lord Jesus Christ, spare me.

Through your holy descent into hell to free captives, Lord Jesus Christ, spare me.

Through your holy resurrection, Lord Jesus Christ, spare me.

Through your holy ascension, Lord Jesus Christ, spare me.

Through the coming of the Holy Spirit, the Paraclete, Lord Jesus Christ, spare me.

3. Prayer to the Trinity

Epheta, that is, be opened [Mk. 7:34].

In the name of our Lord Jesus Christ. Amen, amen, amen.

Repeat three times: Epheta, *to the end.*

Prayer: God Almighty, Father and Son and Holy Spirit, one Trinity and unfathomable unity in three persons, who is and who was and who is to come, I beseech you, exalted majesty, unfathomable and eternal power, that you watch over and defend me, triune truth, single divinity, that you remit all my sins, past, present, imminent, for to you alone are all things possible, as at your word and at your command all things were made and created from nothing, that is, inchoate matter and angels and souls. And as you fashioned the form of all things and the created universe from inchoate matter in six days into their many species and proper forms, so I beseech you, Lord, that you deliver me from mortal sin, and from this mortal condition, and from untimely death, and from all defects of soul and body and their countless spawn.

4. Invocation of the seven days of creation

Deliver me, Lord, you who made light on the first day, and separated it from darkness [Gen. 1:3-4], and day from night, that is, the righteous angels from the sinful ones [Apoc. 12:9], so deign to deliver me from all of Satan's power and the devil's cunning and the snares of demons and the temptations of their accomplices.

Deliver me, Lord, who on the second day fixed the firmament between the upper and the lower waters [Gen. 1:6-8].

Deliver me, Lord, who on the third day fixed the boundary of the sea and earth and caused the dry land to appear and on trees and plants made fruit yielding seed in itself according to its kind [Gen. 1:9-13].

Deliver me, Lord, who on the fourth day made the lights in the firmament of heaven, the sun and the moon and stars, for signs and for seasons and for days and for years [Gen. 1:14-19].

Deliver me, Lord, who on the fifth day made the creeping things and the birds flying above the earth and sea monsters and devised from the waters all manner of living, moving fish and flying things [Gen. 1:20–23].

Deliver me, Lord, who on the sixth day made all manner of beasts and cattle and four-footed animals in their diverse kinds, and formed man from the dust of the earth, breathing into his face the breath of life. Male and female you created them, and you blessed them, saying, "Be fruitful and multiply and fill the earth and rule over the fishes of the sea, and the fowls of the air, and all domestic animals" [Gen. 1:24–31].

Deliver me, Lord, as you on the seventh day blessed all your works, and you sanctified it and caused mankind to rest from all labour, so, deign to bless me, holy and single Trinity, triune divinity, single essence [Gen. 2:1–3].

Merciful, gracious goodness of God, in your infinite mercy defend your creature and remit my sins.[2]

5. Invocation of the nine orders of angels

I entreat you, exalted and infinite goodness, through the holy angelic host, that is, through your holy Angels who recommend and bring word of all lesser matters for the common good to creatures, that is, to mankind.[3]

Deliver me, Lord, by your chief messengers, the Archangels, through whom great tidings are announced to mankind.

Deliver me, Lord, by the holy Virtues, through whom signs and wonders are done at all times.

Deliver me, Lord, by the holy Powers, who command and master the evil spirits, that they not be allowed to work their rage in human affairs as much as they would like, so that their fury may not be accomplished in me.

Deliver me, Lord, by the Principalities, who rule over even the good spirits in fulfilling the divine mysteries.

Deliver me, Lord, by the Dominions who surpass in spiritual power the five aforesaid orders subject to them through obedience.

Deliver me, Lord, by the Thrones, among whom you sit, and through whom you execute your dreadful judgments on creation.

2. Latin has *Elimon*, likely derived from Greek ἐλεήμων (merciful).

3. For Aquinas on the angelic orders, *Summa Theologiae* 1.108, Blackfriars ed. (New York, London, 1964–1981), 14: 121–157. Pierre Salmon, ed., "*Oratio sancti Brendani*," in *Testimonia Orationis Christianæ Antiquioris, Corpus Christianorum Continuatio Mediaevalis* 47 (Turnhout, 1977), 4, cites Gregory the Great, *Homiliarum in Evangelia* 34: 7–14, with which the author of the *Oratio* likely would have been acquainted. See the edition in *Patrologiae cursus completus, Series Latina*, ed. Jacques-Paul Migne (Paris, 1844–1855), 76: 1246–1259, at 1250–1255.

Deliver me, Lord, by the Cherubim, who are the fullness of wisdom and who understand more than rational creatures beneath them, for when they see more astutely in the mirror of divine clarity, they relate the secrets of creation.

Deliver me, Lord, by the glowing or burning Seraphim, who, more rational than any other creature, blaze with love of God, and who so far exceed all creatures in honour that no other spirits come between God and them.

Deliver me, Lord, by these nine orders of holy angels.

6. Invocation of Old Testament deliverances

I beg you, Lord God of compassion and mercy, for pardon and indulgence and remission of all my sins, past, present, and imminent, because you know our nature, for we are flesh and dust. And I beg this gift of you, Lord, through St Peter's patronage and through the blood of Abel your just martyr [Gen. 4:3–10], that you receive the voice of my prayer, as an offering in your praise, as you accepted the pleasing sacrifice of Abel, and that you deliver me from all evil, as you substituted Seth [Gen. 4:25] in his place, from whom the sons of God descended, and as you took Enoch [Gen. 5:24] as he walked with you.

Deliver me, lord, as you delivered Noah in the ark through the flood, together with his household of eight and all living creatures [Gen. 6–7].

Deliver me, Lord, as you delivered all the earth with all its fruits from the flood [Gen. 8].

Deliver me, Lord, as you delivered Heber from the confusion of languages [Gen.11:1–9], in the same way, grant me the merit to evade the peril of sin.[4]

Deliver me, Lord, as you accepted bread and wine, the offering of Melchizedek the priest [Gen. 14:18–20], so deign to accept, Lord, my voice as an offering in your praise. I make a great request of you, Lord, and you know how to grant great things to me, a sinner, not according to my merit but through your bountiful grace: I pray you, Lord, release me daily from transgression.

Deliver me, Lord, as you delivered Abraham from Ur of the Chaldees, and from all trials, and as you were with him always, so do I pray that you never fail to help me [Gen. 12:1–20].

Deliver me, Lord, as you delivered Lot from the Sodomites and enemies [Gen. 19:1–29].

Deliver me, Lord, as you delivered Isaac from death, providing a ram in his place, and as you delivered him from other trials [Gen. 22:1–18].

---

4. St Augustine, *City of God*, Book XVI, Chapter 11, writes that the patriarch Heber's family line preserved the Hebrew language, once common to all humans, amid the confusion of languages God visited on the world because of the presumption of those who built the Tower of Babel. Augustine, *The City of God against the Pagans*, ed. and trans. R.W. Dyson (Cambridge, 1998), 714.

Deliver me, Lord, as you delivered Jacob from the wrath of his brother Esau [Gen. 27:41–45] and from Laban [Gen. 28–31] and he was strong with God [Gen. 32].

Deliver me, Lord, as you delivered Joseph from the envy of his brothers [Gen. 37:1–28] and from the woman's lust, and from slavery and death [Gen. 39], and as you delivered Israel from famine through him [Gen. 45:1–11].

Deliver me, Lord, as you delivered Job from the trials of Satan [Job 1–2] and his own friends [Job 3–37], and as you delivered him from leprosy and then restored to him all his wealth along with living progeny [Job 42]. I entreat you that you likewise deign to restore me to saving health and eternal life.

Deliver me, Lord, as you delivered Moses and Aaron from the might of the Egyptians [Ex. 3:4–22], and as you freed Israel from slavery [Ex. 5, 6:1–8] and from the ten plagues [Ex. 7–12] and from the Red Sea [Ex. 13:17–14:31] and from thirst [Ex. 15:22–25, 17:1–7] and hunger [Ex. 16:1–5] and from battle [Ex. 17:8–16], and as you slew rebels and preserved the loyal [Ex. 32], and as you gave the commandments to the people [Ex. 20]. I entreat you to grant me the gift to know and to understand and to observe your commandments.

Deliver me, Lord, as you delivered Moses and Aaron from the ill will of Israel [Num. 14], and as you delivered Joshua, son of Nun, and Israel through prayer from war with Amalek [Ex. 17:8–16] and Sihon and Og and twenty-nine other kings of the united Canaanite people [Josh. 12].

Deliver me, Lord, as you delivered Phineas and Israel from war, slaying Balak and Balaam [Num. 31:7–8].

Deliver me, Lord, as you delivered Caleb from the treachery of the spies [Num. 13:1–14:38].

Deliver me, Lord, as you delivered Israel and the Ark of the Covenant through the Jordan [Josh. 3].

Deliver me, Lord, as you delivered Rahab from Jericho [Josh. 2, 6].

Deliver me, as you delivered Joshua and Israel when the sun stood still at Gibeon and the moon over the valley of Aijalon [Josh. 10:12–14].

Deliver me, lord, as you delivered Shamgar from the 600 men he slew [Judg. 3:31].

Deliver me, Lord, as you delivered Israel through Deborah's counsel [Judg. 4–5].

Deliver me, Lord, as you delivered Gideon and 300 men from battle with the Midianites [Judg. 7].

Deliver me, Lord, as you delivered Jephthah the Gileadite and Israel from the force of the gentiles [Judg. 11:1–33].

Deliver me, Lord, as you delivered Samson from the lion's mouth – with nothing in his hand he slew it – and as you aided him many times, aid me and I will be saved [Judg. 14:5–6]. And as you preserved Israel's clothes and footwear for forty years [Deut. 29:5], I pray that you likewise in your mercy deign to preserve me and forgive my trespasses.

Deliver me, Lord, as you delivered Ruth from the faithlessness of her [fellow] daughter-in-law [Ruth 1:11–14].[5]

Deliver me, Lord, as you delivered the Ark of the Covenant from Dagon's temple [1 Kings 5–6], and as you delivered Israel through Samuel's prayer [1 Kings 12:14–25], and the Philistines were terrified and driven off by a great noise from heaven [1 Kings 7:10].

Deliver me, Lord, as you delivered David from the fury of the bear and the lion [1 Kings 17:34–37], and from Goliath, defeated with one blow [1 Kings 17:48–51], and from Saul [1 Kings 18:10–12; 19:1, 9–12; 20:31, 33] and from three battles with [giants of] the Philistines [2 Kings 21:15–19], and [as you delivered] Jonathan, son of Saul, and his armour-bearer from the Philistine garrison, for through the power of God 10,000 men were killed by these two [1 Kings 14:1–20; Lev. 26:8].

Deliver me, Lord, as you delivered David's three mightiest men by the well at Bethlehem [2 Kings 23:13–17], and Benaiah, son of Jehoiada, from two lion-like Moabite men, [Benaiah] who killed a lion in a pit on a snowy day and slew an Egyptian with a staff after forcefully wresting a spear from his hand [2 Kings 23:20–21]. And as you delivered the prophet Ahikam, a man of God sent out of Judea to Bethel when the altar was rent, and the king's hand withered [3 Kings 13:1–5].[6]

Deliver me, Lord, as you delivered Elijah the Tishbite of Gilead both from the fury of Ahab and Jezebel [3 Kings 17–19] and from hunger and pursuit by the stream of Cherith [3 Kings 17:1–6]; by his prayer the heavens were stopped from raining for three years and six months [3 Kings 17:1; 18:1], and the widow's jug of oil did not fail nor the jar of meal while God visited his people, [and] he raised her dead son, whom many regard as Jonah rescued a second time from the belly of a whale [3 Kings 17:10–24; Jon. 2:11]. So, Lord, I beseech your great mercy that you deign to rescue me from the deep impurity of my wickedness, for you are my refuge amid the trials that beset me, and absolve me of my sins, past, present and soon to be, for to you alone are all things possible.

---

5. When Ruth's mother-in-law Noemi urges her daughters-in-law Ruth and Orpha to abandon her after Noemi's husband and two sons die, Orpha does leave, but Ruth refuses to forsake her.

6. The Bible passage invoked here refers to "a man of God out of Juda," but does not name him. There is possible confusion with Ahijah in the previous chapter, 1 Kings 12:15, to whom the Lord speaks; Ahikam appears elsewhere, in 4 Kings, 2 Chron., and Jer.

Deliver me, Lord, as you delivered Elijah who slept in the shade of a juniper tree, from pursuit, from hunger, from thirst for forty days and nights without eating [3 Kings 19:1–8].

Deliver me, Lord, as you delivered the third captain of fifty men who fell on his knees beseeching Elijah, after fire from heaven consumed two others [4 Kings 1:9–14].

Deliver me, Lord, as you delivered Elijah, lifted in a chariot of fire [4 Kings 2:11–12].

Deliver me, Lord, as you delivered Elisha crossing the Jordan with a double share of spirit when he called on the God of Elijah [4 Kings 2:9–15], and when he cast salt into the bitter and barren waters at Jericho [4 Kings 2:19–22], and from the forty-two boys in Galgal who taunted him [4 Kings 2:23–24].

Deliver me, Lord, as you delivered Israel through him from thirst during the march of the kings of Israel and Judah [4 Kings 3:6–20], and as you delivered through him from servitude two sons of a widow, multiplying a little oil [4 Kings 4:1–7], and as you brought back through him the son of a woman in a Samarian town [4 Kings 4:33–35], and as you delivered the prophets' sons from death and from hunger when they mistook the wild gourd plants, through flour cast into the pot by the hand of Elisha [4 Kings 4:38–41].[7]

Deliver me, Lord, as you delivered 100 men from hunger with thirty loaves of bread, with many fragments left over [4 Kings 4:42–44].

Deliver me, Lord, as you delivered Naaman, the Syrian king's commander, from leprosy in the Jordan [4 Kings 5:1–14]; as you delivered the prophets' sons from the Jordan's depths just as when the waters came back over the Egyptians at the Lord's command [Josh. 3–4; Ex. 14:26–31]; and as you delivered Dothan, the Samarian town, from the Syrian king's host when the Lord showed Elisha's servant visible blazing bands of angels around Elisha, and then the Syrians were struck down at his prayer and petition [4 Kings 6:1–18].

Deliver me, Lord, as you delivered the Samarian town besieged by King Benhadad, and the Syrian camps were routed by sounds in the night air [4 Kings 7:5–7].

Deliver me, Lord, as you delivered the 100 men from hunger [4 Kings 4:42–44] and revived the corpse of the dead man that touched Elisha's bones in the grave [4 Kings 13:20–21].

Deliver me, Lord, as you delivered Jerusalem and Judaea when 180,000 men of Sennacherib's army were slain in one night by an angel [4 Kings 19:35].

Deliver me, Lord, as you delivered King Hezekiah from death and infirmity, adding fifteen years to his life, when the sun, in a sign, reversed itself by ten lines

---

7. Latin *colloquintidas*, likely for Vulgate *colocyntidas*, wild gourds. 4 Kings 4:39.

[degrees on the sundial] [4 Kings 20:1–11; Is. 38:1–8]. Therefore, I ask, merciful God, that through your abundant power you see fit to constantly cleanse and wash away all my impurities, as you healed the prophet Isaiah from his lips' uncleanness through a Seraph and from many trials [Isa. 6:6–7]. Guard me, Lord, from every evil from the heel of my foot to the crown of my head, within and without.

Deliver me, Lord, as you delivered Jeremiah the prophet from the foulness of the Babylonians and from persecution [Jer. 39:11–40:5].

Deliver me, Lord, as you delivered Daniel the prophet from the fury of the king [Dan. 2:12–49], and from the lions' den [Dan. 6:6–23], and from hunger [Dan. 14:33–38].

Deliver me, as you delivered the three youths Hananiah, Azariah, and Mishael from the furnace of burning fire [Dan. 3:13–50].

Deliver me, Lord, as you delivered Susanna from false witnesses [Dan. 13], and Jonah from the whale's belly [Jon. 2], and as you delivered the Ninevites who repented at Jonah's preaching [Jon. 3].

Deliver me, lord, as you delivered Ezra and Nehemiah and Zerubabel and all Israel from captivity after seventy years [Ezra 2:1–2].

Deliver me, Lord, as you delivered Judas Maccabeus and Israel through the Maccabees in many perils and battles [1 Macc. 3:1–9], when the seven Maccabees with their mother attained martyrdom [2 Macc. 7].

Deliver me, Lord, as you delivered Tobias from blindness [Tob. 11:7–15] and his son from the demon Asmodeus [Tob. 3:7–8] through holy Raphael the Archangel [Tob. 3:24–25].

Deliver me, Lord, as you delivered the Israelites through Queen Esther [Est. 7], and as you delivered Judith and Israel from the hand of Holofernes [Jdt. 13:1–10].

So, forgive me, my God, my great and immoderate crimes and rescue me from mortal sin and from all weaknesses of soul and body past, present, and future, and forgive all the sins of my brothers and sisters, living and dead, and all those from whom I have received alms and favour and for whom I have promised to pray. You, the repayer of all good things, repay those people good things in heaven. Through the grace of your gospel, Lord Jesus Christ, I beseech you, that by the gift of your mercy you grant me indulgence and pardon and remission for all my faults.

Deliver me, Lord, as you delivered Mordecai from the hand of Haman [Est. 6:1–11].

7. Invocation of New Testament deliverances

Deliver me, Lord, as you delivered Zechariah the priest from being mute [Lk. 1:57–64] and Elizabeth from barrenness [Lk. 1:24–25]. So, deign to free me from this mortal condition and from all defects.

Deliver me, Lord, as you delivered the Virgin Mary from all corruption [Mt. 1:18–25] and the three Magi with three gifts from the power of Herod [Mt. 2:1–12].

Deliver me, Lord, as you delivered yourself and Mary and Joseph, fleeing into Egypt, as Herod slew all the boys in Bethlehem and in all its surrounding areas [Mt. 2:13–18]; and as you by yourself delivered the human race [Jn. 1:1–5]; and as you overcame the hostile devil, defeated by you in regard to gluttony, avarice, and pride, through which the first man fell [Mt. 4:1–11]; and as you, coming down from the mountain, delivered the leper from leprosy [Mt. 8:1–3]; and as you healed the gentile centurion's slave in Capernaum [Mt. 8:5–13], and Peter's feverish mother-in-law [Mt. 8:14–15], and in the evening those possessed by demons and all manner of ills [Mt. 8:16–17]; and as you commanded the wind and the sea to be calm [Mt. 8:23–26]; and as you healed two possessed men from an evil army that was driven into [a herd of] swine [Mt. 8:28–32].

Deliver me, Lord, as you delivered the paralysed man borne by four men on a pallet in whom three miracles were obtained: sins were forgiven, [unspoken] thoughts were answered, misfortune was healed with a word [Mt. 9:1–7]. So, deign to act in me, Lord Jesus Christ.

Deliver me, Lord, as you delivered the woman in the street from a flow of blood [Mt. 9:20–22], and as you revived the ruler's dead daughter in the house [Mt. 9:23–25], and as you healed the deaf and mute man from a demon [Mt. 9:32–33], and the withered hand in the synagogue on the Sabbath [Mt. 12:9–13], and the man possessed who was blind and mute [Mt. 12:22].

Deliver me, Lord, as you delivered the 5,000 men, not counting women and children, with five loaves and two fishes, collecting twelve baskets of fragments [Mt. 14:13–21].

Deliver me, Lord, as you delivered Peter as he walked with you on the sea during the fourth watch of the night, and as you commanded the winds and the sea [Mt. 14:22–33], and delivered many with a single command in the fields of Gennesaret [Mt. 14:34–36].

Deliver me, Lord, as you delivered in the region of Tyre the Canaanite woman's daughter who was tormented by a demon, because of her faithful and humble and wise reply [Mt. 15:21–28], and as you refreshed 4,000 men with seven loaves and a few small fishes, with the left over fragments filling seven baskets [Mt. 15:32–38].

Deliver me, Lord, as you delivered them from hunger and sever me from every evil thing, as you lifted Peter and James and John to see your transfiguration on Mount Tabor with Moses and Elijah, where your face shone like the sun and your clothes like snow [Mt. 17:1–5].

Deliver me, Lord, as you delivered someone's epileptic child who at one moment would fall into fire and at another into water, and whom your disciples could not heal [Mt. 17:14–17]. So, deign to cleanse me from all sin of body and soul, and from Adam's sin, and from my own sins and from those of others, just as Simon, casting a hook at your command, found a stater coin [a Tyre silver shekel worth four drachmas] in the fish's mouth and paid the two-drachma [tax, for Jesus and himself] [Mt. 17:23–26].

Deliver me, Lord, as you delivered the deaf and mute man in Decapolis [Mk. 7:31–37]. So, deign to illumine the eyes of my heart and body and my senses, and lead me in the path of your commandments.

Deliver me, Lord, as you illumined the eyes of the two blind men who cried out to you as they came out of Jericho and said, "Have mercy on us, son of David," granting them light [Mt. 20:29–34].

Deliver me, Lord, as you delivered another blind man in Bethsaida [Mk. 8:22–25].

I entreat you, Lord, that you draw me away from the foul impurities of unclean flesh, guiding me to a good death when you direct my soul to leave my body, just as Peter the fisherman who, when he had caught nothing all night, in the morning casting at your word could scarcely draw the net full of fish back to land [Lk. 5:1–7], and as you revived the widow's dead young son from the bier [Lk. 7:11–15].

Deliver me, Lord, as you delivered the woman who washed your feet with tears and dried them with her hair, and you remitted her sins, so, deign to remit all the sins of my body and soul [Lk. 7:36–50].

Deliver me, Lord, as you made upright a woman stooped for eighteen years [Lk. 13:10–13].

Deliver me, Lord, as you cured one afflicted with dropsy on the Sabbath in the house of the chief Pharisee [Lk. 14:1–4].

Deliver me, Lord, as you delivered the ten lepers in a certain village, and sent them to the chief priests, of whom one foreigner returned, giving thanks to God, similarly, merciful Lord God, grant that my lament and my plea be turned into my joy [Lk. 17:11–19]. And as at Cana of Galilee, with your disciples and mother, you transformed six stone water pots filled with water into wine, so deliver me, Lord [Jn. 2:1–10].

Deliver me, Lord, as you revived Lazarus, dead for four days, from four kinds of death: of consciousness and speech and motion and physical destruction. God, grant that I likewise be revived [Jn. 11:1–44].

Deliver me, Lord, as on a festive Sabbath day by the pool of Bethsaida in Jerusalem you delivered the man on a pallet for thirty-eight years who had waited for the waters to be stirred, and he carried away the pallet on the Sabbath through the people [Jn. 5:2–9].

Deliver me, Lord, as you delivered the man blind from birth in Jerusalem by making mud with spittle, smearing his eyes, and bathing his face with water [Jn. 9:1–7], and as you healed the ear of Malchus, the chief priest's servant, cut off by Peter's sword [Jn. 18:10–11; Lk. 22:51], so deign to heal my soul.

And as after your resurrection you raised many bodies of saints who had fallen asleep, deliver me, Lord, as you delivered their souls from hell and rescued them, rising on the third day [Mt. 27:51–53], and after staying with the apostles for forty days amid many proofs, you ascended bodily in a cloud, sitting at the right hand of God the Father [Acts 1:1–11], for you were never not there, so in your kindness deign to intercede for me with the Father to free me; and as you sent the Holy Spirit in fire upon the apostles and 120 souls to cleanse and enlighten them [Acts 2:1–4], so enlighten me from all my impurities.

Deliver me, Lord, as you delivered many people in Peter's shadow from bodily illness [Acts 5:12–16], and as you healed the paralytic man at the ninth hour through Peter [Acts 3:1–10], who had been imprisoned by Herod and, led out by an angel, came back to himself [Acts 12:1–11].

Heal me, Lord, as you healed Aeneas, who lay on a pallet for eight years, through Peter in the north country [Acts 9:32–34], and through him you raised Tabitha from the sleep of death in Joppa [Acts 9:36–40], where Peter in an ecstatic vision was shown a heavenly vessel that contained all things on earth, save humankind [Acts 10:9–15].

Deliver me, Lord, as you delivered Paul from error as he neared Damascus [Acts 9:1–20], and as you revived Eutychus, who died in a fall from an apartment window [Acts 20:9–12], and as you delivered through him [Paul] the father of Publius, who ruled the island of Malta, from dysentery and fever [Acts 28:7–8], so save me, Lord.

Deliver me, Lord, as you saved and delivered Paul on the island of Malta when bitten by a viper [Acts 28:3–5], and as you delivered him when the Jews stoned him almost to death [Acts 14:18–19], and as you restored him to good fortune when he endured shipwreck and was plunged into the depths for three days and nights [Acts 27:27–44].

Deliver me, Lord, as you healed many ailing people who touched his clothing, and as you cast out unclean spirits from the bodies of the possessed [Acts 19:11–16; 16:16–18].

Part II

8. Invocation of the Trinity

I implore you, Lord God Almighty, through your abundant mercy, that you like-wise deign to remit all my sins past, present, and soon to be, for I have sinned against you alone, and to you alone all things are possible. Not according to my deeds do I ask, but according to your indulgence and great compassion.

I entreat you, holy Trinity, single unity, triune truth, God the Father, God the Son, God the Holy Spirit, and through all your works, visible and invisible, and through all your powers and through your words and through all your creatures as well as your ministers and through the holy heavenly host and through all the holy Catholic church from east to west, from north to south: And I pray for your great mercy that you grant me pardon and forgiveness for my sins and that you rescue me at all times even to the end from mortal sin and from defects of soul and body, and that you forgive my brothers and sisters, living and dead, all their sins, especially those for whom I promised to pray.

9. Invocation of Mary, angels, and saints

I entreat you, holy Mary, and I beseech you, nine orders of angels and St Michael and St John the Baptist as well as the twelve apostles Peter, Paul, Andrew, James, John, Thomas, James, Philip, Bartholomew, Matthias, Simon, Thaddeus, Matthew, Mark, Luke, and all the saints of God, that you pray for me to the Lord that he rescue me from all imminent evils and from eternal torment henceforth and forever, through him whose beginning has no end.[8] Amen.

Pray for me, your unworthy servant, holy Mary, virgin most chaste and kind.

St Michael and St Gabriel and St Raphael, holy Thrones, holy Dominions, holy Principalities and Powers, holy Virtues, holy hosts of Cherubim and Seraphim, pray for me a wretch, that through your merits my sins may be remitted by merciful God. Amen.

All holy angels and archangels, all patriarchs and prophets, all holy judges and leaders, all holy kings and Maccabees, all Holy Infants and chosen ones of God, intercede for me.

---

8. The list largely follows the traditional *Litany of the Saints*. Salmon, *Oratio*, xiv–xv, notes that parts of Sections 9 and following are from the Gregorian prayer *Item sabbato in honore omnium sanctorum, Oratio Sancti Gregorii Papae*, in *Patrologiae cursus completus, Series Latina* 101: 585C–586C.

May Christ's nativity,
Christ's circumcision,
Christ's baptism,
Christ's works,
Christ's power,
Christ's teaching,
Christ's preaching,
Christ's cross,
Christ's passion,
Christ's soul,
Christ's flesh,
Christ's spirit,
Christ's resurrection,
Christ's ascension,
the descent and advent of the Holy Spirit the Paraclete
defend me from the cunning snares of the enemy. Amen.

All holy disciples of the Lord, and their holy successors, pray for me,
holy baptizers,
holy archbishops,
holy bishops,
holy priests,
holy deacons,
holy lectors,
holy exorcists,
holy doorkeepers,
holy martyrs,
holy confessors,
holy virgins,
holy anchorites,
holy monks,
holy clerks,
holy layfolk,
holy wives,
holy lords,
holy servants,
holy rich,
holy poor,
holy teachers,
holy artisans.

10. The lorica

May these and all the saints, with the perfect Trinity, be a breastplate for my soul and spirit and body, with all their parts within and without, from sole of foot to crown of head, for sight, sound, smell, taste, touch, flesh, and blood, and for all my bones, nerves and innards, veins and marrow, limbs, and may they keep me from death. For through you, Lord, all my members are brought to life, are given breath, and are healed.

Protect me, Lord, on the right and left, before and behind, below and above, in the air and on the earth, in the water, on the sea, in the tide, in rising, in walking, in standing still, sleeping, waking, in every action, in every place, in every day, in every hour, in every night, in all my life.

Watch over me, come to my aid, triune God, God Almighty, Adonay, Araton, Osya, Eloy, Ely, Eloe, Sabaoth, Elem, Eseria, Saddia, immutable Lord God, and also Emmanuel, Christ Jesus.[9]

Deliver me, Lord God Almighty, from all perils of land and sea and water, and from spectres of all beasts and flying things and four-footed creatures and creeping things.

Defend me, God, from fire, from lightning, from thunder, from hail, from snow, from rain, from wind, from dangers on land, from hurricane, from earthquake, from all evils, from poison, from envy, from evil eyes, from [malicious] words, from the perils of the pit and darkness, from the arrow that flies by day and from the terror that walks by night.

Protect me from all fury that assails the good.

9. Names for God, drawn largely from Greco-Roman, Jewish, Chaldean, and Arabic sources. They appear in the tradition of "learned magic" that spread from Spain and other areas in the twelfth and thirteenth centuries. For example, the *Ars notoria*, from the thirteenth century or earlier, cites in its *Opus operum* version the divine names Sabaoth, Adonay, Eloy, Eloe, Eloa, and Saday, among many others. See Julien Véronèse, ed., *L'Ars notoria au Moyen Âge: Introduction et édition critique* (Florence, 2007), 106; and Claire Fanger, ed., *Invoking Angels: Theurgic Ideas and Practices, Thirteenth to Sixteenth Centuries* (University Park, PA, 2012), 62. The *Liber Iuratus Honorii*, fourteenth century or earlier, refers to Araton among other names. See Fanger, *Invoking Angels*, 7, 172. The *Glossulae super Librum imaginum lunae*, also fourteenth century or earlier, cites the name Seraye. See Sophie Page, *Magic in the Cloister: Pious Motives, Illicit Interests, and Occult Approaches to the Medieval Universe* (University Park, PA, 2013), 83–84, 144.

Part III

11. *The* Confiteor

I confess, and call myself to account before you, my Creator, for all my failings: pride, sevenfold vainglory, and raging anger, despair, and sevenfold avarice, and eightfold gluttony, and fornication, because I am full of these and their affliction. But I repent of these and reject them, and I renounce all my great sins which I have committed in body, in soul, against my neighbour, in thought, in word, in deed. And I write them down in order, that they may be blotted out. And I accuse myself so that you may pardon my sinful wickedness, for I am a sinner and was born in sin, while you, God, truly are without sin.

I entreat the Father through the Son, I entreat the Son through the Father, I entreat the Father and the Son through the Holy Spirit, and through all creatures that praise God with voice and deed, that all vice be removed from me, and all virtues be rooted in me.

Almighty God, in whom all things, through whom all things, by whom all things were made, visible and invisible, hiding the things above and revealing those below, outwardly encompassing and inwardly accomplishing your works, watch over the creature that you formed anew, who has renounced Satan and all his pomps and his works and who believes in you, God the Father, living and true, God Almighty, giving thanks to you for all my life and for all my well-being and for all my innumerable sins of body and soul that I have confessed to you.

I pray to you, Lord, for those who persecute and slander me. Lord, lay not this sin to their charge for they know not what they do.

Deliver me, Lord, from this distress and all evil, from sudden and unforeseen death, before death and at death, from future eternal death, and, after death, from all evil and punishment. Deliver me, God Almighty, and all Christian people.

12. *The commendation*

Lord have mercy, Christ have mercy, Lord have mercy.

Our Father [etc]. I believe in God [etc.].

And commend the one for whom you chant.

Lord God Almighty, maker of heaven and earth, hear favourably my prayer that I have chanted, invoking your generosity, and pleading for your servant, N. [name of the person for whom the prayer is said]. Grant him life and health in this world and, after the passing of his soul, life and eternal rest with all your saints and your grace without end. May the grace of the Holy Spirit enlighten his heart and guide him to eternal life. Amen.

The Judas Episode in the *Navigatio*

Translated from Giovanni Orlandi and Rossanna E. Guglielmetti, *Navigatio sancti Brendani: Alla scoperta dei segreti meravigliosi del mondo* (Florence, 2014), 90–96. This episode is alluded to retrospectively in Chapter 97 of the *R* account. In the common version of the *Navigatio*, it follows the equivalent of *R*'s 59 and precedes 60.

When Brendan had sailed in a southerly direction for seven days, there appeared to them in the sea the form of a man, as it were, sitting on a rock, with a cloth suspended between two iron forks about a cloak's length in front of him; and it was tossed about by the waves like a small boat in danger of shipwreck from a whirlwind. Some of the brothers said it was a bird, others deemed it to be a boat. When the man of God heard them discussing it in such fashion among themselves, he said: "Leave off arguing. Steer the boat to that place." ·

When the man of God drew near the place, the waves all around were motionless, as if curdled. And they came upon a shaggy and disfigured man sitting on a rock. When the waves surged at him from every side, they struck him even to the crown of his head, and when they receded the bare rock on which the wretch sat was exposed. Also, at times the wind blew away the cloth that hung in front of him, at other times it struck his eyes and forehead.

Blessed Brendan asked him who he was, for what fault he was sent there, or why he deserved to undergo such punishment. He said to him: "I am unhappy Judas, the most wretched of deal makers. I am not here because I deserve to be but because of the ineffable mercy of Jesus Christ. It is not counted as a place of punishment to me but of indulgence from the Redeemer in honour of the Lord's Resurrection." For it was then the Lord's Day [Sunday]. "When I sit here, I feel that I am in a paradise of delights compared to my fear of the torments that await me this evening. For day and night, I burn like a mass of molten lead in a cauldron at the centre of the mountain that you have seen [in Chapter 59]. Leviathan [Satan] is there with his cohorts. I was there when it swallowed your brother. And hell was so joyful on that account that it sent forth huge flames. And it so does whenever it devours the souls of the wicked. Yet here I have a place of comfort every Sunday from evening to evening and from Christmas to Epiphany, and from Easter to

Pentecost, and on the Purification and Assumption of the Mother of God. Before and after I am tortured in the depth of hell, along with Herod and Pilate and Annas and Caiaphas. Therefore, I beseech you through the Redeemer of the world that you deign to intercede with the Lord Jesus that I may remain here until daybreak, so that the demons may not torture me on your arrival or lead me away to the evil fate that I purchased in a bad bargain." Brendan said to him: "The Lord's will be done. From tonight until morning, you will not be the morsel of demons."

Again, the man of God questioned him, saying: "What is the meaning of this cloth?" He answered: "I gave this cloth to a leper when I was the Lord's treasurer. But it was not mine to bestow. For it belonged to the Lord and his brothers. And so, I get no comfort from it, but rather affliction. As for the iron forks from which it hangs, I gave them to the temple priests to support their cauldrons. The rock on which I sit, I placed in a ditch in the public road under the feet of passersby before I was a follower of the Lord."

When the hour of vespers had darkened the sea, a countless host of demons covered the face of the deep in a circle, crying out and saying: "Leave us, man of God, for we cannot draw near our companion until you leave him. Nor have we dared to look on our prince's face until we return his friend to him. Give back to us our morsel at once and do not protect him this night." The man of God said to them: "I do not protect him, but the Lord Jesus Christ suffered him to be here this night until morning." The demons said to him: "How do you invoke the Lord's name over him, when he himself is the Lord's betrayer?" The man of God said to them: "I command you, in the name of the Lord Jesus Christ, that you do him no harm until morning."

And so, when the night was over, and the man of God resumed his journey at first light, an infinite host of demons covered the face of the deep, howling and saying: "O man of God, cursed is your coming and your going, for our prince flogged us last night with horrible scourges because we did not bring him that accursed prisoner." The man of God said to them: "Your curse does not concern us, but you yourselves. Whomever you curse is blessed and whomever you bless is cursed."

The demons replied: "Wretched Judas will suffer double punishment for the next six days because you defended him this past night." The venerable father said to them: "You will have no power over that, nor your prince, but God will have the power." And he added: "I command you and your prince in the name of our Lord Jesus Christ not to inflict greater torments on him than before." They answered: "Are you lord of all, that we should heed your commands?" The man of God said to them: "I am his servant, and whatever I order in his name, then I have ministry over those whom he entrusts to me."

And so they followed him until they could no longer see Judas. Then the demons went back and carried off the wretched soul in their midst with great violence and shrieking.

Other Versions of Brendan's *Life*, Latin and Irish

The Latin Tradition

Dubliniensis

The *Vita Sancti Brendani* of the Dublin group, edited by Paul Grosjean and earlier by Patrick Francis Moran, is found chiefly in manuscripts now held in Dublin, but not compiled there.[1] Sharpe suggested that this collection of lives – the "crowning achievement" of hagiography in Ireland – is the work of a redactor at Ferns in Leinster and tentatively dated it to ca. 1230.[2] Kenney, too, held that this *Vita* apparently was "not written in a Brendan community."[3]

The Dublin collection features a *Vita* that arguably is the closest to the Rawlinson *Vita* and shares much material with it. However, it reflects a stronger interest in Irish personal names and topography than other versions. Dublin, like Rawlinson, emphasizes Brendan's connections to Connacht and Clonfert. He

1. They are Marsh's Library, Dublin, MS Z.3.1.5 (formerly V.3.4), fols. 56v–64v, also known as the *Codex Kilkenniensis*; and Trinity College, Dublin, MS 175 (formerly E.3.11), fols. 14r–15v, copied from the same original. Both are fifteenth century. Glyn S. Burgess and Clara Strijbosch, *The Legend of St Brendan: A Critical Bibliography* (Dublin, 2000), 7. For the Marsh's Library version, Paul Grosjean, ed., "Vita S. Brendani Clonfertensis e codice Dubliniensi," *Analecta Bollandiana* 48 (1930): 99–123, here abbreviated as *M*; and Patrick Francis Moran, ed., *Acta Sancti Brendani: Original Latin Documents Connected with the Life of Saint Brendan, Patron of Kerry and Clonfert* (Dublin, 1872). Grosjean edited the *Vita* section of the manuscript from Marsh's Library but omitted the *Navigatio* section. Moran reproduced the *Vita* from Marsh's Library but regarded the *Navigatio* as "imperfect." He printed a separate *Navigatio* based on *La légende latine de S. Brandaines, avec une traduction inédite en prose et en poésie romanes*, ed. Achille Jubinal (Paris, 1836), from Paris, Bibliothèque nationale de France, MS lat. 5572 and BnF MS lat. 3784, checked against BnF MS lat. 2333. Jubinal, *Brandaines*, iv. Moran collated Jubinal's version against the Marsh's Library text and others. Moran, *Acta Sancti Brendani*, 10 n11, 1–26 [*Vita*], 85–131 [*Navigatio*], 27–44 [*Oratio*].

2. Richard Sharpe, *Medieval Irish Saints' Lives: An Introduction to Vitae Sanctorum Hiberniae* (Oxford, 1991), 352, 365, 385. He viewed 1230 as "the latest possible date" (370), and regarded the Dublin *Vita* as the "personal interpretation of a sizeable corpus of older *vitae*" that its author extensively revised (367).

3. James F. Kenney, *The Sources for the Early History of Ireland: Ecclesiastical* (New York, 1929), 413.

directs Iarlaithe to the site for Tuam *in provinchia Connachtorum* (M 108); he receives his monastic rule *in campo An*, at the plain of Mag nAí in Roscommon (M 108); suam civitatem *Cluayn Ferta* (M 116) is described as a *claram civitatem* (M 110) located in Connacht, where he was buried; he founds *Enach Duin ... qui locus est in provinchia Connachtorum* (M 119); a Connacht king offers him land (M 115); he founds a house at Inchiquin in Connacht (M 114–115); and he defends Connacht from attack by Munster (M 119).

However, the Dublin *Vita* is shorter than the Rawlinson account. It takes Brendan's early story to the point where he becomes a priest and monk (M 109) and notes that before his voyage "he founded cells and monasteries in his own region, though not many at the time, and when he returned from his voyage seeking the Promised Land of the Saints, then his *parrochia* (his federation of monasteries) spread across Ireland."[4] The *Navigatio* is then inserted. The story picks up again with Brendan back in Ireland after he has reached his goal, where, in episodes that parallel the Rawlinson account, he founds monasteries (M 109), visits Gildas (M 111–113), and meets Diarmait (M 117–118), and lives out the rest of his days.

Notably, unlike Rawlinson, the Dublin account does not have Brendan relaunching his voyage; the narrative of his time at sea ends with him finding the promised land. There is no mention of a second voyage and further adventures from the *Vita* tradition, including Brendan's encounters with Satan, the giant girl, the forbidden island, the deadly spring, the ravenous rats, the fixed waves, the monstrous cat, and the holy elder. Nor does Dublin relate Brendan's later visit with Brendan of Birr, the tale of Earc's cup, that of the man from Corcumroe, or Colmán the monk's redemption. It also tones down Gildas' grisly vision of Christ's body. This version contains fewer marvellous elements that elevate Brendan's authority and stature and fewer incidents that are doctrinally dubious or embarrassing.

Salmanticensis

The *Vitae* in the *Codex Salmanticensis*, edited by W.W. Heist, are held in the Royal Library of Belgium, Brussels, and once belonged to the Irish College at Salamanca in Spain.[5] They are styled the *Vita prior* or *Codex Salmanticensis*, and the *Vita*

---

4. M 109, my translation.

5. *Codex Salmanticensis*, Brussels, Koninklijke Bibliotheek van België/Bibliothèque Royale de Belgique, MS 7672-74, fols. 69r–77v, early fourteenth century; and KBR, MS 7672-74, fols. 189r–191v, late fourteenth century. Burgess and Strijbosch, *Bibliography*, 4–5. W.W. Heist, ed., *Vitae Sanctorum Hiberniae ex codice olim Salmanticensi nunc Bruxellensi* (Brussels, 1965), *Vita prior* (= S¹) 56–78, *Vita altera* (= S²) 324–331.

altera, respectively. The *Codex Salmanticensis* may have been compiled and kept in an Augustinian house at Clogher in Ulster.[6] Sharpe dated this collection to the fourteenth century, and held that a version of the *Codex Salmanticenis* formed the basis of the Rawlinson conflation.[7]

However, in the Salamanca collection, the *Vita prior* is only nominally a *Vita*. After introducing Brendan and noting that he was Earc's pupil, the author of a rule, the patron of 3,000 monks, and a miracle worker, it picks up the *Navigatio* and does not return to his life story. The *Navigatio* segment largely parallels Rawlinson, but there is no account of the monks' initial, terrifying encounter with Casconius, or of their first visit to the Paradise of Birds. The visit to Ailbhe's island is told only briefly. And the story ends when Brendan reaches his goal; there is no mention of further adventures.

The *Vita altera* is the only Latin *Vita* that does not include substantial *Navigatio* material. It is sharply pared back, and Kenney held it was not written for Brendan's community.[8] As in Rawlinson, Brendan's relaunch is mentioned (*S²* 328). This version presents an abbreviated account of the visit with Gildas (*S²* 329–330), and fleetingly mentions Diarmait in the context of his defeat at the battle of Cúl Dreimne in 561 (*S²* 330–331). It describes Brendan as *de nobilibus parentibus*, of noble family (*S²* 324), and contains Brendan's evocative reply to Brígh's question, "What do you fear, father?" toward the end of his life. "I fear that I am to journey alone, that the way will be dark, I fear an unknown country, the presence of the King, the Judge's sentence" (*S²* 331). And it has Brendan seeking out the region of the Uí Maine, "for that land has need of our ministry. There, perchance, our remains will lie" (*S²* 330).

Vita Anglie

The *Vita Anglie*, edited by Carl Horstman, is found in manuscripts held in London, Oxford, and York.[9] In this version, for the most part bereft of Irish refer-

---

6. Pádraig Ó Riain, "Codex Salmanticensis: A Provenance *inter Anglos* or *inter Hibernos*?," in *"A Miracle of Learning": Studies in Manuscripts and Irish Learning. Essays in Honour of William O'Sullivan*, ed. Toby Barnard et al. (Aldershot, 1998), 91–100, at 98.

7. Sharpe, *Saints*, 296, 391.

8. Kenney, *Sources*, 412.

9. London, British Library, Cotton MS Tiberius E I/1, fols. 128r–134r, fourteenth century; London, British Library, Cotton MS Otho D IX, fols. 40r–46v, fifteenth century; Oxford, Bodleian Library, MS Tanner 15, pp. 75–86, 1499; and York, Minster Library and Archives, MS XVI G 23, fols. 121r–123r, fifteenth century. Burgess and Strijbosch, *Bibliography*, 8. "De sancto Brendano abbate [et confessore]," in *Nova Legenda Anglie: As Collected by John of Tynemouth, John Capgrave, and Others, and First Printed, with New Lives, by Wynkyn de Worde a.d. mdxvi*, ed. Carl Horstman (Oxford, 1901), 136–153.

ences, Brendan is associated in the most general terms with the *occidentali parte Hibernia* (*Anglie*, 136) rather than with Munster or Connacht, and he is buried at *Cluenarca* (*Anglie*, 153). The story of Iarlaithe founding Tuam (*Anglie*, 138) is told without mentioning either name, and Brendan frustrates an attack by *quidam reges Hibernie* against *alteram regionem* without specific mention of the kings of Munster or of the Connacht region (*Anglie*, 153). All this suggests that the intended audience for this life was not primarily Irish.

Indeed, throughout the *Vita Anglie*, the sections recounting Brendan's life are heavily truncated, serving as little more than a summary introduction to an ordinary, shortened *Navigatio*, followed by an even briefer postscript. The story depicts Brendan as a saint of the Church but conveys scant appreciation for his stature as an icon of the Gaelic west of Ireland. The author's interest is chiefly on the voyage, but there, too, the *Vita* voyages are omitted, the *Navigatio* itself is abbreviated, and there is no relaunch. Even so, Kenney regarded this as "the most skilful of all the conflations."[10]

The Irish Tradition

The Irish Lives

Brendan's *Life* in Irish, the *Betha Brénainn*, survives in two principal recensions: the *First Irish Life*, also known as the *Lismore Life*, composed between ca. 1150 and ca. 1190 and likely based on a Latin *Vita* that may have dated to the late 700s; and the *Second Irish Life*, also known as the *Brussels Life*, comprising extracts from Irish recensions of the *Vita Brendani* and the *Navigatio*.[11] In Mac Mathúna's analysis, both the *First* and *Second* Irish lives "represent the same version up to the point where the *First Life* is conjoined with a fragment from *Fis Adomnán* ('The Vision of Adamnán')."[12]

The *First Irish Life*, edited by Whitley Stokes, contains a "reasonably complete" account of Brendan's early life; it refers to the two voyages; and it has the

10. Kenney, *Sources*, 413.

11. Séamus Mac Mathúna, "The *Irish Life of Saint Brendan*: Textual History, Structure and Date," in *The Brendan Legend: Texts and Versions*, ed. Glyn S. Burgess and Clara Strijbosch (Leiden, Boston, 2006), 117–158, at 152, 158, 158 n114.

12. The *First Irish Life*, in University College Cork, the *Book of Lismore* (*Leabhar Leasa Móir*, also known as *Leabhar Mhic Cárthaigh Riabhaigh*), fols. 30v–34v, fifteenth century; the *Second Irish Life*, in Brussels, KBR, MS 4190-200, fols. 224r–263v, a quarto manuscript on paper of 281 folios, largely of saints' lives, written by Mícheál Ó Cléirigh in 1629 from a copy of 1536. Burgess and Strijbosch, *Bibliography*, 9, 11. Séamus Mac Mathúna identified twenty-one manuscripts of the *First Irish Life*, and one of the *Second Irish Life*. Mac Mathúna, "*Irish*

interpolation from the *Fís Adomnán*. However, it does not deal with the saint's later life.[13] It is notable for its description of the Land of Promise as an earthly paradise, and for its homiletic ending.[14]

The *Second Irish Life*, edited by Plummer, is the only version of Brendan's story that rivals the Rawlinson account in amplitude.[15] Plummer concluded that the author was heavily indebted to Latin sources.[16] However, this *Life* also contains additional Irish material. Although lacking the *Fís Adomnán* interpolation, as Mac Mathúna observed, it "consists of alternate extracts from a *Life* identical with the *First Life* and an Irish adaptation of *NB* [the *Navigatio*] which draws on a source similar to that of the Latin *Vita*, S¹ [*Salmanticensis prior*]."[17] For example, it describes how Brendan turned Dobarchú into an otter for killing the saint's oxen, and also how he turned ocean seals into horses to ransom Áed Guaire, a man who had outraged King Diarmait. It relates the traditional tale of the cursing of Diarmait and Tara by St Ruadhán of Lorrha (d. 584), and notes Diarmait's death. And it has Michael the Archangel visiting Brendan in the guise of a sweetly singing bird (*LIS* 2: 79–91). This version relates that "ar 'bá' hé Mícel aingel Brenainn" (Michael was Brendan's angel; *LIS* 1: 92), and credits Michael with telling him to compose the *Oratio*. It also styles Brendan "patruin na pian" (patron of the suffering; *LIS* 1: 87).

Mac Mathúna regarded the *Second Irish Life*, along with the Rawlinson *Vita*, as "the most conflate and complete of all extant versions of the *Life of Brendan*," with the Irish version embodying the final stage of development.[18] Plummer,

---

Life," 119–125. For the *First Irish Life*, see Kenney, *Sources*, 413–414. For the conjuncture, see Mac Mathúna, "*Irish Life*," 117, 125; it occurs at line 3880 in the *First Life* (Whitley Stokes, ed. and trans., "Life of Brenainn son of Finnlug," in *Lives of Saints from the Book of Lismore, Edited with a Translation, Notes, and Indices* [Oxford, 1890; repr. Felinfach, 1995], 260), and at section 151 of the *Second Life* (*LIS* 1: 78). The *Fís Adomnán* is a vision of heaven and hell, credited to Adomnán of Iona, author of the *Life of St Columba*.

13. Mac Mathúna, "*Irish Life*," 131–132. Stokes, *Lives of Saints*, 99–116 [Irish], 247–261 [English].

14. Stokes, *Lives of Saints*, 259–261.

15. Charles Plummer, ed. and trans., *Bethada Náem nÉrenn, Lives of Irish Saints: Edited from the Original MSS. with Introduction, Translations, Notes, Glossary and Indexes* (= LIS) (Oxford, 1922; repr. 1997), 1: xvii, 44–95 [Irish]; 2: 44–92 [English].

16. *LIS* 1: xxii.

17. Mac Mathúna, "*Irish Life*," 136. In Mac Mathúna's analysis, Plummer's Chapters 1–27 of the *Second Irish Life* draw on the *Lismore Life*, then the story draws on the *Navigatio* tradition, returns to the *Life* between 41 and 43, reverts to the *Navigatio* between 43 and the middle of 46, then returns to the *Life* between 46 and 51, followed by the *Navigatio* from 52 to 82, the *Life* from 83 to 96, the *Navigatio* from 97 to 144 and the *Life* from 145 to 209.

18. Mac Mathúna, "*Irish Life*," 136.

too, viewed this *Life* as "the last stage in that process of conflating the various elements of the Brendan story."[19]

The Twelve Apostles of Ireland

Brendan is referred to in Irish in *Dá apstol décc na hÉrenn* (the *Twelve Apostles of Ireland*, i.e, the sixth-century evangelizers) in six manuscripts dating from the fifteenth century to the eighteenth.[20] In his analysis of the *First Irish Life* and the *Twelve Apostles*, Mac Mathúna suggested that the two share material that is not found in the Latin sources, and that the *Twelve Apostles* borrowed from the *Irish Life* tradition.[21] This text places Brendan in the company of Finnian of Clonard, one of Ireland's premier saints and the reputed tutor of the twelve apostles; it casts Brendan as chosen to undertake his sea voyage because he is younger than Brendan of Birr (*LIS* 2: 93); it tells of Brendan calming a whirlpool (*LIS* 2: 94–95); and it presents an extended vision of hell (*LIS* 2: 95–98).

19. *LIS* 1: xvii.

20. Burgess and Strijbosch, *Bibliography*, 11–12. Plummer's edition was based on two manuscripts copied by Mícheál Ó Cléirigh in 1627 and 1634, respectively: Brussels, KBR, MS 2324-40, fols. 70v–71v; and KBR, MS 5100-04, fols. 12r–13r. Burgess and Strijbosch, *Bibliography*, 12. *LIS* 1: xxv, 1: 96–102 [Irish], 2: 93–98 [English].

21. Mac Mathúna, "*Irish Life*," 151.

Saint of the Gaelic West

The Rawlinson *Vita* introduces Brendan as a saint of the peoples of the west of Ireland and especially emphasizes his connection with Connacht.[1] Although Brendan's birthplace is traditionally given as Ciarraige Lúachra in Munster, a region that includes the Alltraige Caille country around Tralee, where his memory is still revered,[2] Rawlinson describes him in general terms as *de Kerraigensium genere* (of the Ciarraige; Chapter 1), of which there were branches in both Munster and Connacht when the manuscript was compiled.[3] The *Vita* has Brendan visit Iarlaithe in Connacht (9); asserts that an angel dictated his monastic rule there on the plain of Mag nAí (10); and records that he evangelized Connacht (11). Later he goes to the "Connacht region" to build his wooden ship (71); has dealings with two Connacht kings, Áed (88) and Diarmait (95); founds houses in Connacht (91); saves Connacht from war (101); and is buried in Connacht at Clonfert (105).

Brendan's influence as an iconic saint of the Gaelic west traced an 800-year arc across the medieval era. His fame was rooted in the ascendancy of Christianity and the advent of monasticism in the sixth century. His foundations and cult were subsequently promoted by powerful Connacht dynasties, as tales of his sanctity and activities assumed literary shape. And his repute was secure amid the arrival of the Anglo-Normans of the twelfth century and the extinction of the

1. The common *Navigatio* emphasizes Brendan's Munster connection, describing him as *Sanctus Brendanus, filius Finlocha nepotis Alti, de genere Eogeni stagni Len regionis Mumenensium ortus fuit* (St Brendan, son of Fionnlugh, descendant of Alte, was born among the Eoganacht of Loch Léin in the land of the people of Munster). Giovanni Orlandi and Rossana E. Guglielmetti, eds., *Navigatio sancti Brendani: Alla scoperta dei segreti meravigliosi del mondo* (Florence, 2014), 2.

2. Pádraig Ó Riain, *A Dictionary of Irish Saints* (Dublin, 2012), 115–116.

3. Tribes of the Ciarraige occupied a prominent place in Connacht; they included the Ciarraige Aí of Cruachu, the Ciarraige Airtich, and another branch to the west. Francis J. Byrne, *Irish Kings and High-Kings* (Dublin, 2004), 236. James F. Kenney, *The Sources for the Early History of Ireland: Ecclesiastical* (New York, 1929), 408. The Annals of Connacht for 1315 tell of a raid made on the Ciarraige of Mag nAí, the Western Ciarraige, and the Ciarraige of Airtech. *AC* 238–241.

Irish high kingship.[4] Brendan's memorializers then elevated him to an unprecedented extent with the creation of the great collections of saints' lives in the thirteenth and early fourteenth centuries.

Born ca. 486 amid a period of rapid Christian conversion in Ireland, and within roughly a generation of Patrick's death (d. 461) – well within living memory – Brendan would live to see Ireland ruled by a Christian high king from Connacht, Diarmait mac Cerbaill (r. 544–565). Down through the centuries, kings of Munster and Connacht associated themselves and their dynasties with Brendan's name and foundations. They used such ties to enhance their status as princes, to assert political and religious interests, to demarcate territory, and to contend with foreign intrusion. They vied for control of and patronized Clonfert, which became an important centre soon after its foundation ca. 558~564, employing it for international diplomacy, for church gatherings, and for peace brokering. The foundation was a centre of Gaelic culture, Latin scholarship, and ecclesiastical reform.

From ancient times, Brendan was associated with Connacht rulers and with forebears of the Ua Conchobair [O'Connor] dynasty. In 744, the Connacht king Forggus mac Cellaig (d. 756) of the Uí Briúin Aí affirmed the importance of Clonmacnoise and of Clonfert by imposing a *lex Ciarani ... et lex Brendani* in honour of their founders on areas under his control across both sides of the Shannon at Longford.[5] The laws granted royal protection to monasteries, enforcement of their rights and privileges, and immunities. By 800, when Muirgius mac Tommaltaig (r. 786–815) of the Uí Briúin Aí was in power,[6] Brendan's fame was assuming literary shape; the early *Vita* and *Navigatio* likely were composed around that time. From Muirgius' grandson Conchobar (d. 882) came the Ua Conchobair dynasty that dominated east Connacht in the tenth to early thirteenth centuries and that patronized Clonfert and other foundations along the Shannon.

Under Toirrdelbach Ua Conchobair (r. 1106–1156), the first Connacht king to hold the high kingship of Ireland, Connacht became a national power, dominating Munster and other regions prior to the Anglo-Norman arrival of 1169. Toirrdelbach's military prowess, far-reaching campaigns, and success in divid-

---

4. Brendan was a "very popular" saint even among the English of Ireland in the heavily colonized "four obedient shires" of Dublin, Meath, Louth, and Kildare. Sparky Booker, *Cultural Exchange and Identity in Late Medieval Ireland: The English and Irish of the Four Obedient Shires* (Cambridge, 2018), 1, 139–140.

5. Byrne, *Irish Kings*, 252. *AU* 198–199.

6. Byrne, *Irish Kings*, 251.

ing his enemies secured him the high kingship from 1120.[7] During his reign he "transformed the face of Connacht," and he "traversed Ireland as no king before him had ever traversed it." In addition to building castles at Dunmore, Galway, Athlone, Ballinasloe, and Collooney, he partitioned Munster, maintained cavalry and a fleet of ships, built bridges across the Shannon to provide ready access to neighbouring regions, and diverted the course of the river Suck to create a flood plain to bolster Connacht's natural defences.[8]

In his drive to assert Connacht's and his own importance, Toirrdelbach cultivated political loyalty and support from Brendan's devotees and houses, and from associated churches, in areas allied to him. He patronized Tuam, near Dunmore as well as Clonmacnoise and Roscommon; built churches, round towers, and ecclesiastical enclosures; and erected high crosses.[9] Early in Toirrdelbach's reign, at the Synod of Ráith Bressail in 1111, Brendan's church at Clonfert was recognized as the diocese of the Uí Máine kingdom.[10] When the Irish church won papal recognition as a national institution, and four archdioceses were established, Toirrdelbach had the status of Tuam raised to that of a Gaelic archiepiscopal see at the Synod of Kells-Mellifont in 1152, reflecting his supremacy and confirming Connacht's political and ecclesiastical importance.[11]

7. Griffin Murray, *The Cross of Cong* (Dublin, 2014), 30–31. The annals in 1156 memorialize Toirrdelbach: "Toirdhealbhach Ua Conchobhair, King of Connaught, Meath, Breifne, and Munster, and of all Ireland with opposition, flood of the glory and splendour of Ireland, the Augustus of the west of Europe, a man full of charity and mercy, hospitality and chivalry, died after the sixty-eighth year of his age, and was interred at Cluain-mic-Nois, beside the altar of Ciaran, after having made his will, and distributed gold and silver, cows and horses, among the clergy and churches of Ireland in general." *Annala rioghachta Eireann: Annals of the Kingdom of Ireland, by the Four Masters*, ed. and trans. John O'Donovan (Dublin, 1851; repr. New York, 1966), 2: 1118–1119.

8. F.J. Byrne, "The Trembling Sod: Ireland in 1169," *NHI* 2: 1–42, at 36. J.A. Watt, *The Church and the Two Nations in Medieval Ireland* (London, New York, 1970), 52. Emmet O'Byrne, "Ua Conchobair, Tairrdelbach (1088–1156)," in *Medieval Ireland: An Encyclopedia*, ed. Seán Duffy et al. (New York, 2005), 471–474.

9. The Connacht kings also promoted the cult of St Patrick locally to emulate and counter the influence of Armagh. While Armagh claimed authority over Patrician pilgrimage sites and sources of wealth such as Croagh Patrick and Patrick's Well at Ballintubber Abbey, Connacht princes and clerics resisted, and asserted their own control. Murray, *Cross*, xxxi, 41.

10. Aubrey Gwynn and R. Neville Hadcock, *Medieval Religious Houses, Ireland* (London, 1970), 64, 153.

11. Byrne, "Trembling Sod," 42. Armagh was awarded primacy. Cashel was awarded Munster. Dublin was newly recognized as an archdiocese, as was Tuam, with jurisdiction over Clonfert and Annaghdown. Ó Riain, *Dictionary*, 116.

Toirrdelbach commissioned prestige objects for the principal churches in his sphere of influence.[12] Although Brendan's foundations at Clonfert and Ardfert, while ancient, seem to have possessed no comparable relics, what his houses did have, in the *Vita* and *Navigatio* traditions that long predated their compilation in the great collections of saints' lives, were venerable and widely acclaimed tales of his sanctity, miracles, and travels that came to be featured prominently in those collections. This period produced "a significant impetus toward hagiographical production, whether in celebration of formal diocesan status or in the demand for such recognition on historic grounds," Sharpe noted.[13] The Brendan traditions, glorifying him and associating him with Patrick and other saints, served to help sustain Ua Conchobair prestige, to promote and celebrate Tuam, and to enhance the repute of Clonfert diocese and its churches. Insofar as Brendan and his far-reaching influence were identified with Ua Conchobair political jurisdiction, these traditions added lustre to the court. Ultimately, they proved to be durable literary artefacts that would survive long after the religious relics of the day had been destroyed or lost.

Toirrdelbach and his line, like princes before them, would have had reason to foster Brendan's cult, among those of other saints. Not only was Brendan a celebrated figure who had roots and devotees in both Connacht and Munster, Ua Conchobair spheres of influence, his authority had by then "spread across Ireland," in the words of the Dublin account of his life.[14] He also had achieved international recognition as the hero of the *Navigatio*. Brendan's story, largely set in Toirrdelbach's domains, and associating Brendan with ancient Connacht rulers and Ua Conchobair forebears, and with Tuam, affirmed Toirrdelbach's stature, advanced his policy of promoting Tuam as a metropolitan see, and celebrated Clonfert as an episcopal see and pilgrimage site, generating prestige and wealth. Just as the earlier *Tripartite Life of Patrick* had associated Patrick with Armagh, Brendan was given a role as the prophetic founder of Iarlaithe's church at Tuam, emblematic of Connacht princely rule and clerical dignity.[15] The prominence

12. Murray, *Cross*, 210–211. In 1123, Toirrdelbach paraded a relic of the True Cross across the country, enshrining a fragment of it in the Cross of Cong, held at Roscommon. His patronage ensured that Tuam archdiocese had a relic to rival Armagh's Bachall Ísu (the Staff of Jesus) and other relics; and he appears to have given Cashel a small fragment of the True Cross as well. Dublin, too, had its fragment. Murray, *Cross*, 208–209, 216.

13. Richard Sharpe, *Medieval Irish Saints' Lives: An Introduction to Vitae Sanctorum Hiberniae* (Oxford, 1991), 33.

14 Paul Grosjean, ed., "Vita S. Brendani Clonfertensis e codice Dubliniensi," *Analecta Bollandiana* 48 (1930): 99–123, at 109.

15. Whitley Stokes, ed. and trans., *The Tripartite Life of Patrick* (London, 1887; repr. 1965), 1: 228–231, 252–253.

accorded Brendan's legend in the later collections of lives that featured Patrick and other high-status saints appears to reflect Connacht's ascendancy and dominance in the twelfth century, when "a fair amount of hagiographical activity" was taking place.[16]

Early in the reign of Toirrdelbach's son Ruaidrí (r. 1156–1183), who succeeded him as the last high king, the relics of Bishop Maoineann and of Cuimín Fada "were removed from the earth by the clergy of Brenainn, and they were enclosed in a protecting shrine" in 1162, evidence of Clonfert's significance as a diocesan centre and pilgrimage site in an age of pilgrimage.[17] Burnt in 1164, the cathedral was rebuilt in 1167, and again around 1180.[18]

By then, Ireland was changed utterly. The Anglo-Norman invasion instigated a struggle for political legitimacy that consumed the twelfth and thirteenth centuries, bringing to much of Ireland, including the west, "chronic warfare, racial conflict in church and the wider society, legal inequity and severe social disruption."[19] Yet even after the Anglo-Norman arrival, Clonfert continued to be a centre of political and religious significance. In 1175, Abbot Canthordis of Clonfert helped negotiate the Treaty of Windsor between Henry II, the Angevin king of England, and Toirrdelbach's son Ruaidrí confirming the latter's high kingship in areas outside of Henry's direct jurisdiction in exchange for his fealty. Ruaidrí ruled over an autonomous though much-reduced kingdom in Connacht, under vassalage to the English crown, the only Irish kingdom to have even semi-independent status.[20] Four years later, in 1179, Lorcán Ó Tuathail [Laurence O'Toole], the archbishop of Dublin and papal legate, presided over a reformist synod at Clonfert leading up to the extraordinary installation of Ruaidrí's nephew Tommaltach Ua Conchobair, a Connacht man, as archbishop of Armagh, the

16. Sharpe, *Saints*, 29.

17. Marie Therese Flanagan, *The Transformation of the Irish Church in the Twelfth and Thirteenth Centuries* (Woodbridge, 2010), 222. *AFM* 2: 1144–1147.

18. The church is noted for its Romanesque doorway and east window. It occupies an elevated spit on a curve of the Shannon with the river on three sides and was the site of a medieval bishop's palace, a woodland, and a yew walk in the shape of a cross. Nearby is a site identified as the former Augustinian priory of St Mary de Portu Puro. Dermot Nolan, and Pat Ruane, *St Brendan's Cathedral, Clonfert, County Galway: Conservation Plan* (Dublin, 2004), 10, 12.

19. Donnchadh Ó Corráin, *The Irish Church, Its Reform and the English Invasion* (Dublin, 2017), 116.

20. Dáibhí Ó Cróinín, *Early Medieval Ireland, 400–1200* (London, 1995), 289. Also, F.X. Martin, "Overlord Becomes Feudal Lord, 1172–85," *NHI* 2: 98–126, at 106–107. Edmund Curtis, *A History of Medieval Ireland from 1086 to 1513* (New York, London, 1938; repr. 1968), 68–69. Nicholas Vincent, "Angevin Ireland," in *Cambridge History of Ireland, Vol. 1, 600–1550*, ed. Brendan Smith (Cambridge, 2018), 185–221, at 188.

see of Patrick, and primate of all Ireland.[21] Later, in 1190, Clonfert hosted a bid to broker peace between the Connacht king Cathal Crobderg, Ruaidrí's brother, and Cathal Carrach, Ruaidrí's grandson.[22]

During this era, Ua Conchobair princes, with other leaders of the native Irish, resisted and pushed back the Anglo-Norman settlement. As did Ruaidrí, they negotiated with the English crown and with Anglo-Norman magnates to have their local lordships recognized in exchange for fealty and, at times, homage, and to buy a measure of autonomy and peace.[23] Ann Dooley characterized this period as a time "when the end of Gaelic kingship as a serious construct of western medieval Christendom was not yet envisaged."[24] The earliest of the extant Latin lives, the *Vita Brendani* of the Dublin collection, was likely composed and compiled during this era.

In Colin Veach's estimation, "the first eight decades of English involvement in Ireland could in many ways be characterised as a protracted struggle to control Connacht."[25] While Ruaidrí and Toirrdelbach's other sons Conchobair Máenmaige (r. 1183–1189) and Cathal Crobderg (r. 1189–1224) ruled for nearly seven decades, the kingdom's integrity endured, despite the Norman settlement, and the Ua Conchobair may well have aspired to establish themselves as hereditary custodians of a national monarchy.[26] Indeed, as late as the reign of Áed mac Fedlimid Ua Conchobair (r. 1265–1274), Cathal Crobderg's grandson, Ua Conchobair princes held effective power regionally. Áed's death in 1274 plunged Gaelic Connacht into chaos and civil war for the next half century.[27] Between 1274 and 1315 there were no fewer than thirteen kings of Connacht, most of whom were killed or deposed by their own kinsmen or followers.[28] In

21. Martin, "Overlord," 119–120.

22. *AFM* 3: 88–89.

23. F.X. Martin, "Allies and an Overlord, 1169–72," *NHI* 2: 67–97, at 88–89. And James Lydon, "The Expansion and Consolidation of the Colony, 1215–54," *NHI* 2: 156–178, at 163.

24. Ann Dooley, "The Date and Purpose of *Acallam na Senórach*," *Éigse* 34 (2004): 97–126, at 123.

25. Colin Veach, "Conquest and Conquerors," in *Cambridge History of Ireland*, ed. Smith, 1: 157–182, at 168.

26. Byrne, "Trembling Sod," 33–34, 36. Ó Cróinín, *Early Medieval Ireland*, 286.

27. The annals for 1274 famously memorialize Áed as a king "who wasted and desolated Connacht in fighting the Galls and Gaels who opposed him; a king who inflicted great defeats on the Galls and pulled down their palaces and castles; a king who took the hostages of the Ui Briuin and the Cenel Conaill; the destroyer and healer of Ireland was he." *AC* 160–163.

28. Goddard Henry Orpen, *Ireland Under the Normans 1169–1333* (Oxford, 1920; repr. Dublin, 2005), 487. James Lydon, "A Land of War," *NHI* 2: 240–274, at 249.

1316, William de Burgh's decisive victory at Athenry over Fedlimid Ua Conchobair (r. 1310–1316) "quenched the greatest hope for a century of restoring a Gaelic kingdom"; the Ua Conchobair "'kingdom of Connacht' was henceforth but an empty name."[29]

Amid this political eclipse, Clonfert remained a site of religious and cultural significance well into the thirteenth and fourteenth centuries.[30] And Brendan continued to be revered as an icon of the Gaelic west. The clerics who compiled the Rawlinson B 485 manuscript ca. 1300 gave pride of place to Brendan's *Vita* in its most imaginative and extended form in Latin, a legend that commemorated him both as a great saint of the Gaelic west, and as a native son whose story and foundations identified him with Ua Conchobair political power, territorial claims, and wider aspirations. Like the Dublin *Vita* but grander in conception and scope, the *Vita Sancti Brendani* of the Oxford collection reflected not only the interests of Brendan's religious community, but also those of its secular patrons. In the twilight of Ua Conchobair rule, on the frontier of Connacht not far from Clonfert, Brendan's memorializers associated him with Irish princes of a golden, imagined past and their ambitious successors, and honoured him as a champion of the peoples of the west.

29. Curtis, *History*, 189. Even so, fully a third of Ireland including much of Connacht, West Munster, and parts of Ulster continued to maintain Gaelic customs and traditions during this era. J.A. Watt, "Approaches to the History of Fourteenth-Century Ireland," *NHI* 2: 303–313, at 311–312. And R.E. Glasscock, "Land and People, *c.* 1300," *NHI* 2: 205–239, at 225. Moreover, Brendan continued to be associated with the preservation of Gaelic dynastic lines well into the fourteenth century. The *Book of Magauran*, late fourteenth century, features a poem to Tomás Mág Shamhradháin, died 1343, in which a king and his wife fast against Brendan to ensure that the queen's unborn child will be a son, maintaining the dynasty. The *Book of Uí Maine*, also late fourteenth century, contains a legend of a pregnant royal widow petitioning Brendan to ensure that her unborn child is a boy after her husband is killed in battle; Brendan changes the unborn child, a girl, into a boy. See Lambert McKenna, ed., *The Book of Magauran: Leabhar Méig Shamhradháin* (Dublin, 1947), viii. Poem XVIII, 140–153 [Irish], 343–347 [English]. And Pádraig Ó Riain, "Two Legends of the Uí Máille," *Éigse* 14 (1971/72): 1–12.

30. During this period Clonfert continued to be associated with leading clerics, scholars, and poets. In 1266, a cleric from Rome, John de Alatro, was named bishop of Clonfert and papal nuncio. Great Britain, Public Record Office, *Index to Ancient Correspondence of the Chancery and the Exchequer*, Vol. 1, A–K, Lists and Indexes, Supplementary Series 15A (New York, 1969), 15. The Annals of the Four Masters for 1259 record the death of Cormac O'Luimlin, "Bishop of Clonfert-Brendan, and the most illustrious man in Ireland for wisdom." *AFM* 3: 372–373. In 1328, they record the death of Maurice O'Gibellan, "Chief Professor of the New Law, the Old Law, and the Canon Law, a truly profound philosopher, a learned poet, and a canon chorister of Tuam, Elphin, and Achad-Chonaire, Killala, Annadown, and Clonfert, the official and the general Brehon [judge] of the archbishopric." *AFM* 3: 536–537.

Bibliography

Primary Sources

Adomnán of Iona. *Adomnán's Life of Columba*. Ed. and trans. Alan Orr Anderson and Marjorie Ogilvie Anderson. London: Nelson, 1961. Rev. ed. Marjorie Ogilvie Anderson. Oxford: Clarendon Press, 1991.

—. *Life of St Columba*. Trans. Richard Sharpe. London: Penguin, 1995.

Augustine. *The City of God against the Pagans*. Ed. and trans. R.W. Dyson. Cambridge: Cambridge University Press, 1998.

Barron, W.R.J., and Glyn S. Burgess, eds. *The Voyage of Saint Brendan: Representative Versions of the Legend in English Translation*. Exeter: University of Exeter Press, 2002.

Bede. *Bede's Ecclesiastical History of the English People*. Ed. Bertram Colgrave and R.A.B. Mynors. Oxford: Clarendon Press, 1969.

Benedeit. *The Anglo-Norman Voyage of St Brendan*. Ed. Ian Short and Brian S. Merrilees. Manchester: Manchester University Press, 1979.

Benedict. *The Rule of St. Benedict, In Latin and English with Notes*. Ed and trans. Timothy Fry. Collegeville, MN: Liturgical Press, 1981.

Best, Richard Irvine, and Hugh Jackson Lawlor, eds. *The Martyrology of Tallaght: From the Book of Leinster and MS. 5100–4 in the Royal Library, Brussels*. London: Henry Bradshaw Society, 1931.

Bili. *The Old English Life of Machutus*. Ed. David Yerkes. Toronto: University of Toronto Press, Centre for Medieval Studies, 1984.

Brendan. "*Oratio Sancti Brendani*." Ed. Pierre Salmon. In *Testimonia Orationis Christianæ Antiquioris*, ed. Petrus Salmon, Carolus Coebergh, and Petrus de Puniet, vii–xxxvii, 1–31. Corpus Christianorum Continuatio Mediaevalis 47. Turnhout: Brepols, 1977.

Carey, John, trans. *King of Mysteries: Early Irish Religious Writings*. Dublin: Four Courts Press, 1998.

Cawley, A.C., and J.J. Anderson, eds. *Pearl, Cleanness, Patience, Sir Gawain and the Green Knight*. London: Dent, 1962; repr. 1976.

Cummian. *Cummian's Letter De Controversia Paschali*. Ed. Maura Walsh and Dáibhí Ó Cróinín. Toronto: Pontifical Institute of Mediaeval Studies, 1988.

Dooley, Ann, and Harry Roe, trans. *Tales of the Elders of Ireland: Acallam na Senórach*. Oxford: Oxford University Press, 1999.

Edgar, Swift, and Angela M. Kinney, eds. *The Vulgate Bible, Douay-Rheims Translation*. 6 vols, 7 parts. Cambridge, MA: Harvard University Press, 2010–2013.

Freeman, A. Martin, ed. *Annála Connacht: The Annals of Connacht (A.D. 1224–1544)*. Dublin: Dublin Institute for Advanced Studies, 1944; repr. 1970.

Great Britain. Public Record Office. *Index to Ancient Correspondence of the Chancery and the Exchequer*. Vol. 1, A–K. Lists and Indexes: Supplementary Series (Public Record Office), 15A. New York: Kraus Reprint, 1969.

Haddan, Arthur West, and William Stubbs, eds. *Councils and Ecclesiastical Documents Relating to Great Britain and Ireland*. 3 vols. Oxford: Clarendon Press, 1869–1878; repr. 1964.

Hanson, R.P.C. *Saint Patrick: Confession et lettre à Coroticus*. Paris: Éditions du Cerf, 1978.

Heist, W.W., ed. *Vitae Sanctorum Hiberniae ex codice olim Salmanticensi nunc Bruxellensi*. Brussels: Société des Bollandistes, 1965.

Hennessy, William M., and Bartholomew MacCarthy, eds. and trans. *Annala Uladh = Annals of Ulster, Otherwise Annala Senait, Annals of Senat: A Chronicle of Irish Affairs from A.D. 431 to A.D. 1540*. 4 vols. Dublin: Her Majesty's Stationery Office, 1887–1901.

Horstman, Carl, ed. "De sancto Brendano abbate [et confessore]." In *Nova Legenda Anglie: As Collected by John of Tynemouth, John Capgrave, and Others, and First Printed, with New Lives, by Wynkyn de Worde a.d. mdxvi*, 1: 136–153. Oxford: Clarendon Press, 1901.

Jubinal, Achille. *La légende latine de S. Brandaines, avec une traduction inédite en prose et en poésie romanes*. Paris: Techener, 1836.

Mac Airt, Seán, ed. and trans. *The Annals of Inisfallen: MS. Rawlinson B. 503*. Dublin: Dublin Institute for Advanced Studies, 1951; repr. 1977.

Mac Airt, Seán, and Gearóid Mac Niocaill, eds. *The Annals of Ulster (to A.D. 1131): Part I: Text and Translation*. Dublin: Dublin Institute for Advanced Studies, 1983.

Martyrologium Romanum: Gregorii papae XIII iussu editum, Urbani VIII et Clementis X auctoritate recognitum, ac deinde anno MDCCXLIX Benedicti XIV opera ac studio emendatum et auctum. Rome: Typis Polyglottis Vaticanis, 1948.

McKenna, Lambert, ed. *The Book of Magauran: Leabhar Méig Shamhradháin*. Dublin: Dublin Institute for Advanced Studies, 1947.

—, ed. *Dán Dé. The Poems of Donnchadh Mór Ó Dálaigh, and the Religious Poems in the Duanaire of the Yellow Book of Lecan*. Dublin: Educational Company of Ireland, 1922.

Moran, Patrick Francis, ed. *Acta Sancti Brendani: Original Latin Documents Connected with the Life of Saint Brendan, Patron of Kerry and Clonfert*. Dublin: William Bernard Kelly, 1872.

O'Donovan, John, trans. *Annála Rioghachta Éireann: Annals of the Kingdom of Ireland, by the Four Masters, from the Earliest Period to the Year 1616*. 7 vols. Dublin: Hodges, Smith, 1851; repr. New York: AMS Press, 1966.

O'Meara, John J., trans. *The Voyage of Saint Brendan: Journey to the Promised Land: Nav-*

igatio Sancti Brendani Abbatis. Dublin: Dolmen Press, 1976; Gerrards Cross: Colin Smythe, 1991.

O'Rahilly, Cecile, ed. *Táin bó Cúailnge: Recension I*. Dublin: Dublin Institute for Advanced Studies, 1976.

Ó Riain, Pádraig, ed. *Beatha Ailbhe: The Life of Saint Ailbhe of Cashel and Emly*. London: Irish Texts Society, 2017.

—, ed. *Beatha Bharra: Saint Finbarr of Cork: The Complete Life*. London: Irish Texts Society, 1994.

—, ed. *Corpus Genealogiarum Sanctorum Hiberniae*. Dublin: Dublin Institute for Advanced Studies, 1985.

—, trans. *Four Offaly Saints: The Lives of Ciarán of Clonmacnoise, Ciarán of Seir, Colmán of Lynally and Fíonán of Kinnitty*. Dublin: Four Courts Press, 2018.

—, trans. *Four Tipperary Saints: The Lives of Colum of Terryglass, Crónán of Roscrea, Mochaomhóg of Leigh and Ruadhán of Lorrha*. Dublin: Four Courts Press, 2014.

Orlandi, Giovanni, ed. *Navigatio sancti Brendani*. Milan, Varese: Istituto Editoriale Cisalpino, 1968.

Orlandi, Giovanni, and Rossana E. Guglielmetti, eds. *Navigatio sancti Brendani: Alla scoperta dei segreti meravigliosi del mondo*. Florence: SISMEL Edizioni del Galluzzo, 2014.

—, eds. *Navigatio Sancti Brendani: Editio maior*. Florence: SISMEL Edizioni del Galluzzo, 2017.

Patrologiae cursus completus, Series Latina. Ed. J.-P. Migne. 221 vols. Paris, 1844–1855.

Plummer, Charles, ed. *Bethada náem nÉrenn, Lives of Irish Saints: Edited from the Original MSS. with Introduction, Translations, Notes, Glossary and Indexes*. 2 vols. Oxford: Clarendon Press, 1922; repr. 1997.

—, ed. *Vitae Sanctorum Hiberniae: Partim hactenus ineditae ad fidem codicum manuscriptorum recognovit prolegomenis notis indicibus instruxit*. 2 vols. Oxford: Clarendon Press, 1910; repr. Dublin: Four Courts Press, 1997.

Prosper of Aquitaine. *Epitoma Chronicon*. Ed. Theodore Mommsen. In *Monumenta Germaniae Historica: Auctores Antiquissimi 9: Chronica Minora*, 1: 341–485. Berlin: Weidmannsche, 1892.

Radner, Joan Newlon, ed. *Fragmentary Annals of Ireland*. Dublin: Dublin Institute for Advanced Studies, 1978.

Salmon, Pierre. *See under* Brendan.

Selmer, Carl, ed. *Navigatio Sancti Brendani Abbatis: From Early Latin Manuscripts*. Notre Dame: University of Notre Dame Press, 1959; repr. Dublin: Four Courts Press, 1989.

Stokes, Whitley, ed. and trans. "The Annals of Tigernach (Being Annals of Ireland, 807 B.C. to A.D. 1178)." *Revue Celtique* 16 (1895): 374–419; *Revue Celtique* 17 (1896): 6–33, 119–263, 337–420; *Revue Celtique* 18 (1897): 9–59, 150–198, 267–303.

—, ed. and trans. *Félire Óengusso Céli Dé = The Martyrology of Oengus the Culdee*. London: Henry Bradshaw Society, 1905; repr. Dublin: Dublin Institute for Advanced Studies, 1984.

—, ed. and trans. "Life of Brenainn, Son of Finnlug." In *Lives of Saints from the Book of Lis-*

more, ed. Whitley Stokes, 99–116 (Irish); 247–261 (English). Oxford: Clarendon Press, 1890; repr. Felinfach: Llanerch, 1995.

—, ed. and trans. *The Tripartite Life of Patrick (Bethu Phátraic): with Other Documents Relating to the Saint*. 2 vols. London: Her Majesty's Stationery Office, 1887; repr. Wiesbaden: Kraus Reprint, 1965.

Thomas Aquinas. *Summa Theologiae: Latin Text and English Translation, Introductions, Notes, Appendices and Glossaries*. Blackfriars ed. 61 vols. New York: McGraw-Hill; London: Eyre & Spottiswoode, 1964–1981.

Véronèse, Julien, ed. *L'Ars notoria au Moyen Âge: Introduction et édition critique*. Florence: SISMEL Edizioni del Galluzzo, 2007.

Webb, J.F., trans. "The Voyage of St Brendan." In *Lives of the Saints*, 31–68. Harmondsworth: Penguin Books, 1965; repr. 1973.

Wimbledon, Thomas. *Wimbledon's Sermon Redde rationem villicationis tue: A Middle English Sermon of the Fourteenth Century*. Ed. Ione Kemp Knight. Duquesne Studies, Philological Series 9. Pittsburgh: Duquesne University Press, 1967.

Secondary Sources

Abram, Andrew. "Augustinian Canons and the Survival of Cult Centres in Medieval England." In *The Regular Canons in the Medieval British Isles*, ed. Janet Burton and Karen Stöber, 79–95. Turnhout: Brepols, 2011.

Barnard, Toby, Dáibhí Ó Cróinín, and Katharine Simms, eds. *'A Miracle of Learning': Studies in Manuscripts and Irish Learning, Essays in Honour of William O'Sullivan*. Aldershot: Ashgate, 1998.

Bartlett, Thomas, et al. *The Cambridge History of Ireland*. 4 vols. Cambridge: Cambridge University Press, 2018.

Bieler, Ludwig. "Two Observations Concerning the *Navigatio Brendani*." *Celtica* 11 (1976): 15–17. Repr. in *The Otherworld Voyage in Early Irish Literature*, ed. Jonathan M. Wooding, 91–93. Dublin: Four Courts Press, 2000; repr. 2014.

Boardman, Steve, John Reuben Davies, and Eila Williamson, eds. *Saints' Cults in the Celtic World*. Woodbridge: Boydell Press, 2009.

Booker, Sparky. *Cultural Exchange and Identity in Late Medieval Ireland: The English and Irish of the Four Obedient Shires*. Cambridge: Cambridge University Press, 2018.

Brown, Raymond E., Joseph A. Fitzmyer, and Roland E. Murphy, eds. *The New Jerome Biblical Commentary*. Englewood Cliffs, NJ: Prentice Hall, 1990.

Burgess, Glyn S., and Clara Strijbosch. *The Brendan Legend: Texts and Versions*. Leiden, Boston: Brill, 2006.

—. *The Legend of St Brendan: A Critical Bibliography*. Dublin: Royal Irish Academy, 2000.

Burton, Janet, and Karen Stöber, eds. *The Regular Canons in the Medieval British Isles*. Turnhout: Brepols, 2011.

Byrne, Francis J. *A Thousand Years of Irish Script: An Exhibition of Irish Manuscripts in Oxford Libraries.* Oxford: Bodleian Library, 1979.

—. *Irish Kings and High-Kings.* London: B.T. Batsford, 1973. 2nd ed. Dublin: Four Courts Press, 2001; repr. 2004.

—. "The Trembling Sod: Ireland in 1169." In *A New History of Ireland*, ed. T.W. Moody et al., 2: 1–42.

Carey, John. "Saint Patrick, the Druids, and the End of the World." *History of Religions* 36, no. 1 (1996): 42–53.

—. "The Sea and the Spirit: Two Notes." In *Gablánach in Scélaigecht: Celtic Studies in Honour of Ann Dooley*, ed. Sarah Sheehan, Joanne Findon, and Westley Follett, 26–37. Dublin: Four Courts Press, 2013.

—. "Varieties of Supernatural Contact in the Life of Adamnán." In *Studies in Irish Hagiography: Saints and Scholars*, ed. John Carey, Máire Herbert, and Pádraig Ó Riain, 49–62. Dublin: Four Courts Press, 2001.

—, Máire Herbert, and Pádraig Ó Riain, eds. *Studies in Irish Hagiography: Saints and Scholars.* Dublin: Four Courts Press, 2001.

Carney, James. "*A maccucáin, sruith in tíag.*" *Celtica* 15 (1983): 25–41.

—. "Language and Literature to 1169." In *A New History of Ireland*, ed. T.W. Moody et al., 1: 451–510.

—. "Review of *Navigatio Sancti Brendani Abbatis*, Edited with Introduction and Notes by Carl Selmer." *Medium Ævum* 32 (1963): 37–44. Repr. in *The Otherworld Voyage*, ed. Wooding, 42–51. Dublin: Four Courts Press, 2000; repr. 2014.

Charles-Edwards, T.M. *Early Christian Ireland.* Cambridge: Cambridge University Press, 2000.

Clancy, Thomas Owen. "Subversion at Sea: Structure, Style and Intent in the *Immrama*." In *The Otherworld Voyage*, ed. Wooding, 194–225. Dublin: Four Courts Press, 2000; repr. 2014.

Curtis, Edmund. *A History of Medieval Ireland from 1086 to 1513.* London: Methuen; New York: Barnes & Noble, 1938; repr. 1968.

Despy, Georges. "Le scriptorium de l'abbaye de Waulsort au XIe siècle: La provenance du psautier-hymnaire Munich, Bayer. Staatsbibl. Clm. 13067." *Le Moyen Age* 59 (1953): 87–115.

Dooley, Ann. "The Date and Purpose of *Acallam na Senórach*." *Éigse* 34 (2004): 97–126.

Downham, Clare. *Medieval Ireland.* Cambridge: Cambridge University Press, 2018.

Duffy, Seán, Ailbhe MacShamhráin, and James Moynes, eds. *Medieval Ireland: An Encyclopedia.* New York: Routledge, 2005.

Dumville, David N. "Two Approaches to the Dating of *Nauigatio Sancti Brendani*." *Studi Medievali* 29 (1988): 87–102. Repr. in *The Otherworld Voyage*, ed. Wooding, 120–132. Dublin: Four Courts Press, 2000; repr. 2014.

Esposito, Mario. "An Apocryphal 'Book of Enoch and Elias' as a Possible Source of the *Navigatio Sancti Brendani*." *Celtica* 5 (1960): 192–206. Repr. in *The Otherworld Voyage*, ed. Wooding, 27–41. Dublin: Four Courts Press, 2000; repr. 2014.

Fanger, Claire, ed. *Invoking Angels: Theurgic Ideas and Practices, Thirteenth to Sixteenth Centuries.* University Park: Pennsylvania State University Press, 2012.

Flanagan, Marie Therese. *The Transformation of the Irish Church in the Twelfth and Thirteenth Centuries.* Woodbridge: Boydell Press, 2010.

Follett, Westley. *Céli Dé in Ireland: Monastic Writing and Identity in the Early Middle Ages.* Woodbridge: Boydell Press, 2006.

Frame, Robin. "Ireland after 1169: Barriers to Acculturation on an 'English' Edge." In *Norman Expansion: Connections, Continuities and Contrasts*, ed. Keith J. Stringer and Andrew Jotischky, 115–141. Farnham, Surrey: Ashgate, 2013.

Freeman, Philip. *St. Patrick of Ireland: A Biography.* New York: Simon & Schuster, 2004.

Glasscock, R.E. "Land and People, c. 1300." In *A New History of Ireland*, ed. T.W. Moody et al., 2: 205–239.

Gougaud, Louis. "Étude sur les *loricae* celtiques et sur les prières qui s'en rapprochent." *Bulletin d'ancienne littérature et d'archéologie chrétiennes* 1 (1911): 265–281; 2 (1912): 33–41, 101–127.

—. *Les Saints irlandais hors d'Irlande: Étudiés dans le culte et dans la dévotion traditionnelle.* Louvain: Bureau de la Revue; Oxford: Blackwell, 1936.

Grabowski, Kathryn, and David Dumville, eds. *Chronicles and Annals of Medieval Ireland and Wales: The Clonmacnoise-Group Texts.* Woodbridge: Boydell Press, 1984.

Grosjean, Paul. "Vita S. Brendani Clonfertensis e codice Dubliniensi." *Analecta Bollandiana* 48 (1930): 99–123.

Gwynn, Aubrey, and R. Neville Hadcock. *Medieval Religious Houses, Ireland: With an Appendix to Early Sites.* London: Longman, 1970.

Hayes-McCoy, G.A. "The Completion of the Tudor Conquest and the Advance of the Counter-Reformation, 1571–1603." In *A New History of Ireland*, ed. T.W. Moody et al., 3: 94–141.

Herren, Michael W. "Patrick, Gaul, and Gildas: A New Lens on the Apostle of Ireland's Career." In *Gablánach in Scélaigecht: Celtic Studies in Honour of Ann Dooley*, ed. Sarah Sheehan, Joanne Findon, and Westley Follett, 9–25. Dublin: Four Courts Press, 2013.

Hughes, Kathleen. *The Church in Early Irish Society.* London: Methuen, 1966.

—. "The Church in Irish Society, 400–800." In *A New History of Ireland*, ed. T.W. Moody et al., 1: 301–330.

—. "A Manuscript of Sir James Ware: British Museum Additional 4788." *Proceedings of the Royal Irish Academy* 55 (1952/1953): 111–116.

Jahner, Jennifer, Emily Steiner, and Elizabeth M. Tyler, eds. *Medieval Historical Writing: Britain and Ireland, 500–1500.* Cambridge: Cambridge University Press, 2019.

Kenney, James F. *The Sources for the Early History of Ireland: Ecclesiastical: An Introduction and Guide.* New York: Columbia University Press, 1929.

Lydon, James. "The Expansion and Consolidation of the Colony, 1215–54." In *A New History of Ireland*, ed. T.W. Moody et al., 2: 156–178.

—. "The Impact of the Bruce Invasion, 1315–27." In *A New History of Ireland*, ed. T.W. Moody et al., 2: 275–302.

—. "A Land of War." In *A New History of Ireland*, ed. T.W. Moody et al., 2: 240–274.

Mac Mathúna, Séamus. "The *Irish Life of Saint Brendan*: Textual History, Structure and Date." In *The Brendan Legend: Texts and Versions,* ed. Glyn S. Burgess and Clara Strijbosch, 117–158. Leiden, Boston: Brill, 2006.

—. "The Structure and Transmission of Early Irish Voyage Literature." In *Text und Zeittiefe*, ed. Hildegard L.C. Tristram, 313–357. Tübingen: Gunter Narr, 1994.

Mackley, J.S. *The Legend of St Brendan: A Comparative Study of the Latin and Anglo-Norman Versions*. Leiden, Boston: Brill, 2008.

Martin, F.X. "Allies and an Overlord, 1169–72." In *A New History of Ireland*, ed. T.W. Moody et al., 2: 67–97.

—. "Diarmait Mac Murchada and the Coming of the Anglo-Normans." In *A New History of Ireland*, ed. T.W. Moody et al., 2: 43–66.

—. "Overlord Becomes Feudal Lord, 1172–85." In *A New History of Ireland*, ed. T.W. Moody et al., 2: 98–126.

McManus, Damian. "An Elegy on the Death of Aodh Ó Conchobhair († 1309)." *Ériu* 51 (2000): 69–91.

McNamara, Martin. "*Navigatio Sancti Brendani*: Some Possible Connections with Liturgical, Apocryphal and Irish Tradition." In *The Brendan Legend: Texts and Versions,* ed. Glyn S. Burgess and Clara Strijbosch, 159–191. Leiden, Boston: Brill, 2006.

Moody, T.W., F.X. Martin, F.J. Byrne, W.E. Vaughan, Art Cosgrove, J.R. Hill, and Dáibhí Ó Cróinín, eds. *A New History of Ireland*. 9 vols. Oxford: Oxford University Press, 1976–2011.

Murray, Griffin. *The Cross of Cong: A Masterpiece of Medieval Irish Art*. Dublin: Irish Academic Press, 2014.

Ní Mhaonaigh, Máire. "Perception and Reality: Ireland *c.*980–1229." In *The Cambridge History of Ireland, Vol. 1, 600–1550*, ed. Brendan Smith, 131–156. Cambridge: Cambridge University Press, 2018.

Nolan, Dermot, and Pat Ruane. *St Brendan's Cathedral, Clonfert, County Galway: Conservation Plan*. Dublin: Heritage Council, 2004.

O'Byrne, Emmet. "Ua Conchobair, Tairrdelbach (1088–1156)." In *Medieval Ireland: An Encyclopedia*, ed. Seán Duffy et al., 471–474. New York: Routledge, 2017.

Ó Corráin, Donnchadh. *The Irish Church, Its Reform and the English Invasion*. Dublin: Four Courts Press, 2017.

Ó Cróinín, Dáibhí. *Early Medieval Ireland. 400–1200*. London: Longman, 1995.

—. "Ireland, 400–800." In *A New History of Ireland*, ed. T.W. Moody et al., 1: 182–234.

Ó Cuív, Brian. *Catalogue of Irish Language Manuscripts in the Bodleian Library at Oxford and Oxford College Libraries: Part 1, Descriptions*. Dublin: Dublin Institute for Advanced Studies, School of Celtic Studies, 2001.

Ó Donnchadha, Gearóid. *St Brendan of Kerry, the Navigator: His Life and Voyages*. Dublin: Open Air, Four Courts Press, 2004.

O'Donnell, Thomas. "Monastic History and Memory." In *Medieval Historical Writing: Britain and Ireland, 500–1500*, ed. Jennifer Jahner, Emily Steiner, and Elizabeth M. Tyler, 35–50. Cambridge: Cambridge University Press, 2019.

O'Donoghue, Denis. *Brendaniana: St Brendan the Voyager in Story and Legend*. Dublin: Browne and Nolan, 1893; repr. as *Lives and Legends of Saint Brendan the Voyager*. Felinfach: Llanerch, 1994.

O'Hanlon, John. "St. Brendan, Brandon or Brenainn, Bishop and Patron of Ardfert, County of Kerry, and of Clonfert, County of Galway." In *Lives of the Irish Saints: With Special Festivals, and the Commemorations of Holy Persons, Compiled from Calendars, Martyrologies, and Various Sources, relating to The Ancient Church History of Ireland*, 5: 389–472. Dublin: James Duffy and Sons, 1875.

Ó Riain, Pádraig. "Codex Salmanticensis: A Provenance *inter Anglos* or *inter Hibernos*?" In *'A Miracle of Learning': Studies in Manuscripts and Irish Learning. Essays in Honour of William O'Sullivan*, ed. Toby Barnard, Dáibhí Ó Cróinín, and Katharine Simms, 91–100. Aldershot: Ashgate, 1998.

—. *A Dictionary of Irish Saints*. Dublin: Four Courts Press, 2012.

—. "Two Legends of the Uí Máille." *Éigse* 14 (1971/72): 1–12.

Orpen, Goddard Henry. *Ireland Under the Normans 1169–1333*. Oxford: Clarendon Press, 1920; repr. Dublin: Four Courts Press, 2005.

Page, Sophie. *Magic in the Cloister: Pious Motives, Illicit Interests, and Occult Approaches to the Medieval Universe*. University Park: Pennsylvania State University Press, 2013.

Parente, Pietro, Antonio Piolanti, and Salvatore Garofalo. *Dictionary of Dogmatic Theology*. Trans. Emmanuel Doronzo. Westminster, MD: Christian Classics, 1974.

Plummer, Charles. "On Two Collections of Latin Lives of Irish Saints in the Bodleian Library, Rawl. B. 485 and Rawl. B. 505." *Zeitschrift für celtische Philologie* 5, no. 1 (1905): 429–454.

—. "Some New Light on the Brendan Legend." *Zeitschrift für celtische Philologie* 5 (1905): 124–141. Repr. in *The Otherworld Voyage*, ed. Wooding, 1–14.

Selmer, Carl. "The Runic Inscription of *Codex Latinus Monacensis* 13067." *Publications of the Modern Language Association* 53, no. 3 (1938): 645–655.

Sharpe, Richard. *Medieval Irish Saints' Lives: An Introduction to Vitae Sanctorum Hiberniae*. Oxford: Clarendon Press, 1991.

Sheehan, Sarah, Joanne Findon, and Westley Follett, eds. *Gablánach in Scélaigecht: Celtic Studies in Honour of Ann Dooley*. Dublin: Four Courts Press, 2013.

Simms, Katharine. "The Political Recovery of Gaelic Ireland." In *The Cambridge History of Ireland, Vol. 1, 600–1550*, ed. Brendan Smith, 272–299. Cambridge: Cambridge University Press, 2018.

Smith, Brendan, ed. *The Cambridge History of Ireland, Vol. 1, 600–1550*. Cambridge: Cambridge University Press, 2018.

Strijbosch, Clara. *The Seafaring Saint: Sources and Analogues of the Twelfth Century Voyage of Saint Brendan*. Trans. Thea Summerfield. Dublin: Four Courts Press, 2000.

Stringer, Keith J., and Andrew Jotischky, eds. *Norman Expansion: Connections, Continuities and Contrasts*. Farnham, Surrey: Ashgate, 2013.

Tristram, Hildegard L.C., ed. *Text und Zeittiefe*. Tübingen: Gunter Narr, 1994.

Veach, Colin. "Conquest and Conquerors." In *The Cambridge History of Ireland, Vol. 1, 600–1550*, ed. Brendan Smith, 157–182. Cambridge: Cambridge University Press, 2018.

Vinaver, Eugène. *The Rise of Romance*. Oxford: Clarendon Press, 1971.

Vincent, Nicholas. "Angevin Ireland." In *The Cambridge History of Ireland, Vol. 1, 600–1550*, ed. Brendan Smith, 185–221. Cambridge: Cambridge University Press, 2018.

Wakefield, Walter L., and Austin P. Evans, trans. *Heresies of the High Middle Ages*. New York, London: Columbia University Press, 1969.

Watt, J.A. "The Anglo-Irish Colony under Strain, 1327–99." In *A New History of Ireland*, ed. T.W. Moody et al., 2: 352–396.

—. "Approaches to the History of Fourteenth-Century Ireland." In *A New History of Ireland*, ed. T.W. Moody et al., 2: 303–313.

—. *The Church and the Two Nations in Medieval Ireland*. London, New York: Cambridge University Press, 1970.

—. *The Church in Medieval Ireland*. Dublin: Gill and Macmillan, 1972.

—. "Gaelic Polity and Cultural Identity." In *A New History of Ireland*, ed. T.W. Moody et al., 2: 314–351.

Wooding, Jonathan M. "The Date of *Nauigatio S. Brendani abbatis*." *Studia Hibernica* 37 (2011): 9–26.

—. Introduction to John J. O'Meara's translation in "The Latin Version." In *The Voyage of Saint Brendan. Representative Versions of the Legend in English Translation*, ed. W.R.J. Barron and Glyn S. Burgess, 13–25. Exeter: University of Exeter Press, 2002.

—. "The Medieval and Early Modern Cult of St Brendan." In *Saints' Cults in the Celtic World*, ed. Steve Boardman, John Reuben Davies, and Eila Williamson, 180–204. Woodbridge: Boydell Press, 2009.

—, ed. *The Otherworld Voyage in Early Irish Literature*. Dublin: Four Courts Press, 2000; repr. 2014.

Index of Manuscripts

General Index

Henry II, English king (r. 1154–1189) 114
heresy 15, 25 with n79, 78
hermits 14, 39, 40–41, 72–75 with n80
and n82, 83–84 with n120. *See also*
Paul the hermit
high kingship 15, 21, 22, 80 n105, 110–
112, 114
Horstman, Carl 106
Hughes, Kathleen 2, 8 n44

Iarlaithe of Tuam, saint 11, 16, 37, 38
with n19, 105, 107, 110, 113
Íde of Killeedy, saint 11, 14, 15, 16 with
n57, 24, 34 with n7, 37, 71 with n74, 76
with n89, 80
Immram Máel Dúin 18
Inchiquin (Brendan foundation) 2 n7,
15, 22, 24, 78, 79, 105
Inishdadroum (Brendan foundation) 2
n7, 14, 15, 75, 79
invocations in prayer: of angels 28, 29,
89–90, 98; of Christ 29, 87–88, 95–98,
99; of Mary 29, 98; of the Trinity 28,
29, 88, 98
Isle of Delight 40–43, 68–69. *See also*
Ternoc
Isle of Sheep 12, 46–47, 55
Isle of Steadfast Men 13, 20, 59–60

John de Alatro, bishop of Clonfert 116
n30
Jonah 58, 92, 94
Judas 15, 17, 25, 65 n62, 83 with n119,
102–103

Kells-Mellifont, synod of 38 n20, 112
Kenney, James F. 17, 104, 106, 107

Lateran, Fourth Council of 24–25
lex Brendani 111
Life of Columba: see under Adomnán
Life of St Brendan: anchor, marvellous 14,
72, 74, 75; birth miracles 4 n16, 11, 25,

33–34; bondage, man freed from 23, 24,
79–80; Brendan's death 15, 18, 27, 85–
86; column, crystal 13, 20, 63 with n60;
evangelization, acts of 11, 19, 22, 39,
110; demonic smiths 13, 64; fasting 39–
40, 43, 44 n38, 51, 61, 75, 81; fleas,
plague of 14, 24, 75; fog 13, 41, 42, 67–
68; forbidden island 70, 105; grapes, isle
of 13, 61; gryphon attack 13, 20, 61–62;
herald 14, 71–72; Ireland, return to 13,
14, 15, 17, 68–69, 75; maiden chastised
11, 24, 35–36; sea beasts 13, 20, 24, 25,
30, 58–59; seasonal travels 47, 51, 57;
second voyage 14, 17, 20, 24, 69 n70,
70–75 with n74, 105, 106, 107; stone,
man turned to 11, 23, 25, 26, 36–37
with n15; youth drowned 14, 22, 24,
75–76, 77; youth revived 11, 15, 39. *See
also* angels; boat; Casconius; Corcumroe, man from; demons; Earc of Alltraige: cup; Faithful Steward; hell; Isle
of Delight; Isle of Sheep; Isle of Steadfast Men; Judas; marvels and wonders;
miracles; monks; monsters; Paradise of
Birds; Paul the hermit; power, acts of;
Promised Land of the Saints; prophesy;
providence; Satan; visions and dreams.
See also Brendan of Clonfert and Ardfert; *Vita Sancti Brendani*
Life of St Malo: see under Bili
Lismore Life of Brendan: see *First Irish Life*
litany, litanies 28, 29, 98 n8; *Litany of Pilgrim Saints* 3–4
Longford 8, 111
Lorcán Ó Tuathail (Laurence O'Toole),
archbishop and saint 114
lorica 27–30, 100
Lyons, Second Council of 25

Mac Mathúna, Séamus 5, 107 with n12,
108 with n17, 109
Macc Ardae mac Fidaig, Cíarraige
Lúachra king (fl. 486) 34 with nn4–5